Chinatown Britain

Steve Lau

Published by
Chinatown Online

www.chinatown-online.co.uk

First published by Chinatown Online, 2002

www.chinatown-online.co.uk

ISBN 0-9542556-0-7

Printed in the United kingdom

Photograph credits
Pages 30, 34 Hong Kong Tourist Association
Page 108 & 109 Birmingham City library
Page 118 & 119 Newcastle Library Service
Page 8 Royal Collection, Windsor
Page 4, 5 Tower Hamlets Library Services
Page 8 Jonathan Yee
Page 54 Amoy (HP Foods)

献给我的父亲和同时代的人。
他们这一代克苦经营，在英国
建立起一个成功而有活力的华
人社区。

Dedicated to my
father and all his
contemporaries
who worked
long and hard to
establish within
one generation a
successful and
vibrant Chinese
community in
the UK.

Acknowledgments

Putting together something like Chinatown Britain is a long and drawn out process, and it would be unfair to claim all the credit.

Most special thanks to Andy, colleague, friend and confidant, for encouraging me to see the project through, for being honest enough to tell me when things didn't quite seem right, and humble enough to accept there were some things I wanted just so. Andy also edited and proof read the text way beyond the call of duty, and as though this were not enough, acted as technical adviser on some of the finer points of preparing the project for print.

My thanks go too to Mr Wing Yip for his support, encouragement and even the odd editorial pointer.

Thanks to John the eternal optimist: we got there in the end. To Ann-Marie for the final proofing. To Hsiao Hung and Stanley for translation works.

Contents

Foreword

Britain's Chinatowns bear testament to the hard work and determination of the Chinese. Chinatown Britain is both an informative guide book and a celebration of the achievements of the Chinese community in Britain.

Great Britain has become a truly multi-racial, multi-cultural society, and nowhere is this more evident than in Britain's vibrant Chinatowns. From the grandeur of Liverpool's Imperial Arch (the largest outside of China) to the moments of quiet to be found in London Chinatown's pagoda, the Chinese have made an incredible impression wherever they have settled.

Although Chinatowns are often brash, noisy places, they are in fact a great anomaly in the general picture of the Chinese in Great Britain who have

often been called the 'hidden minority'. An authoritative history of the Chinese in Britain is conspicuous by its absence. Much work has been undertaken to document the arrival and settlement of African Caribbean and Indian subcontinent immigrants in Britain, but no published works are available about the Chinese. In part this book addresses that absence, and does so in a colourful, vibrant way.

Birmingham, Liverpool, London, Manchester and Newcastle all boast a well established Chinatown. All have their own distinct characteristics, while at the same time a certain reassuring similarity. This book gives a unique insider's guide to all five Chinatowns as well as a well balanced, intelligent look at the Chinese in Great Britain.

Chinatown Online

網上中國城

GERRARD STREET W1

www.chinatown-online.co.uk

Chinatown Online is the UK's premiere web site on all things Chinese. This unique website is a huge resource featuring hundreds of pages covering everything from chop suey to feng shui, tai chi to Taiwan, Mao to Macau, kung fu to tofu. Visit us and find out even more.

英國
中國
城

Newcastle
Page 117

Manchester
Page 79

新堡

Birmingham
Page 107

曼徹斯特

利物浦

Liverpool
Page 91

伯明翰

倫敦

London
Page 57

The Chinese Arrive

Limehouse Causeway, original home to London's Chinatown. 1911.

The recorded arrival of the Chinese in Britain goes as far back as 1681 (see page 8). It was another 100 years before the Chinese were to arrive in any number, but arrive they did - as sailors. By 1800 there were up to 500 Chinese sailors in London at any given time. They were all transient, exclusively male, and employees of the East India Company. It was not until the mid 1800s that Chinese began to settle in Britain, where they settled in the dock areas of Liverpool and Limehouse in London.

At the turn of the 1800s China was resisting all attempts by the outside world to get her to participate in international trade. The Chinese saw European wool cloth as inferior to silk, and their earthenware inferior to Chinese porcelain. British and European goods were indeed inferior to the Chinese, and so the Chinese saw little advantage in trading.

British merchants were particularly keen for the Chinese to trade as they had discovered a lucrative market for tea in Britain. Although the Chinese were willing to sell tea, there were no goods that the Chinese wanted in return. This lead to a heavy trade deficit, until the British introduced a new product which became heavily in demand: opium. Grown in Bengal by the British East India Company, opium was exported to China and traded for tea. Tea was exported to Britain and great profits made.

Understandably the Chinese were not happy at the opium trade– trading in opium had been made illegal in China in 1729. Although Chinese merchants and corrupt officials were implicated in the trade as middlemen, the Chinese Emperor was adamant that the trade should stop, and appointed a commissioner, Lin Zexu to put an end to it. In 1839 Lin Zexu seized and destroyed 12,500 tons of British opium. The British reacted with military might, forcing China to trade by the terms of peace of what became known as the First Opium War (1840 – 1842). A second war broke out in 1860, in which British and French troops destroyed the Imperial Winter Palace in Beijing and forced a complete opening of China to foreign trade.

Although the success of the British in the Opium Wars lead to an increased degree of contact between Britain and China, the Chinese population in Britain remained very, very small. At the turn of the 20th century there were just five hundred and forty-five permanent Chinese residents in Britain, almost exclusively male. They ran small shops and cafés, catering for Chinese sailors that came into and sailed out of London, Cardiff and Liverpool.

By 1914 there were some 30 Chinese businesses in the Limehouse area of London, which had become known as Chinatown. The British were, however, far from welcoming. In particular, Chinese sailors were considered a direct threat to their British counterparts - in 1908 British seamen formed a picket at the East India Dock to prevent Chinese crews from signing on for work.

The Chinese were almost universally suspected of being lawless opium addicts who were unkempt and dirty: a strange stereotype considering that up until the 1950s the most successful laundries in London were wholly owned and operated by the Chinese.

Public perceptions of the Chinese were much improved by a Hollywood epic of 1919. D W Griffith's *Broken Blossoms* portrayed a young Chinese poet as an unassuming hero, rescuing an English maiden in distress from her murderous father.

The postwar years in Britain posed a major threat for the Chinese in Britain. The Limehouse area of East London was obliterated during the blitz on London, and Liverpool docks had been badly bombed. At the same time the decline in British shipping resulted in the Seaman's Union changing its rules, making it far more difficult for non-British seamen to find work at British ports. The laundry industry also went into terminal decline with the introduction of high street launderettes and the appearance of domestic washing machines.

This picture of a Chinese funeral in 1911 shows how the Chinese have always organised their own affairs, and taken care of each other. The 'collars' being worn are of a 'tong' or mutual aid society. The rabbi to the left of the picture was present as the law required an 'ordained' person to be there, but he did nothing at all during the proceedings.

As late as 1950 there were still only some two thousand Chinese in Britain. The Chinese faced a real threat with the decline of their traditional trades, and were seeking new income opportunities as well as a place to live. This bleak situation was turned around by a new phenomenon in Britain: returning soldiers from the war in the Far East suddenly created a new customer base for Chinese cuisine. The catering trade provided new employment opportunities for a wave of post war immigration into Britain which continued until the early 1970s.

The Chinese built economic success on the back of the catering industry, but equally, this basis for their economic success lead to a phenomenon unique in British immigrant communities - widespread geographical dispersion. Whilst this has created five Chinatowns, it has also meant that the Chinese can be found in every corner of the British Isles, from the remote Hebridean Islands to the Channel Isles, from Ulster to East Anglia.

The next major wave of Chinese came in the early to mid 1980s with the arrival in the UK of a large number of "Vietnamese boat people". Although originating from Vietnam, over 80% of the Vietnamese refugees were ethnic Chinese. The Chinese had fled Vietnam following the forced closure of Chinese schools and factories and the imposition of heavy meeting and travel restrictions by the new administration after the Vietnam war in 1975.

With the reversion of Hong Kong to Chinese sovereignty in 1997, many had predicted a mass influx of Chinese into the UK after some 50,000 Chinese families were given British citizenship. This, however, never materialised as those who said the Chinese could not make Hong Kong work were proven wrong.

Most Chinese in Britain come from Hong Kong, and within that grouping there is a large proportion who are from the Hakka community (see opposite). In addition sizeable numbers have come from Malaysia, Singapore, the Chinese mainland and Vietnam. These account for about 88% of the Chinese in Britain, the rest come from around 80 other countries.

The Chinese have become Britain's most successful immigrant community – although this is a rarely flaunted fact. The Chinese community's total weekly household income exceeds that of all other ethnic groups, and weekly earnings of Chinese in full-time employment exceeds that of all other ethnic groups, except white men who earn the same as Chinese men. Meanwhile, the Chinese are the highest academic achievers, with 1 in 4 having a university degree.

Today there are over 10,000 Chinese restaurants and takeaways in the UK; but that's not their only contribution to the nations wellbeing. Chinese are increasingly moving into other businesses including insurance, travel, accountancy, law and other technical professions. At the same time the Chinese are making an impact on such essential services as health, medicine, social care, scientific research and information technology that is way beyond what would be expected from their relatively low numbers.

Hakka woman in traditional dress

The Hakka are the earliest inhabitants of Hong Kong, and as such it is of little surprise that there are large a number of Hakka in the UK.

The Hakka originally occupied central China, and are believed to be one of the earliest settlers in China. The Hakka moved south, to Jiangxi, Fujian, and Guangdong provinces to avoid the dilution of their culture.

Hakka culture and traditions have been preserved in language, customs and food, and in some cases have marked them out from the wider Chinese population: the Hakka for example, staunchly refused to adopt the practice of foot binding.

Hakka literally means "Guests", and was the name given to the Hakka when they moved south. Traditionally an agricultural people, over the last hundred years or so Hakka people have migrated to all corners of the earth.

With a tradition of migration, the Hakka have historically had to struggle to survive in new lands, and they are rightly known for their perseverance, even in the most adverse of conditions.

Shen Fu-Tsung

The first recorded Chinese person in Britain (and indeed in Europe) was Shen Fu-Tsung. Shen Fu-Tsung was born of Chinese Christian parents and followed his parents' faith. Although he kept his Chinese name, it was pre-fixed with the Christian names Michael Alphonsus. In 1681 Shen Fu-Tsung accompanied the Jesuit priest Father Philip Couplet, Procurator of the China Jesuits in Rome, to Europe. Shen Fu-Tsung visited Italy and France before arriving in England.

While in England he became known at the court of James II, and indeed, his portrait was painted for the King by Sir Godfrey Kneller. The portrait is described by the naval surgeon, James Yonge (who saw Shen Fu-Tsung at Windsor Castle in July 1687) as "being done very well like him."

Shen Fu-Tsung made good use of his time in England, working in the Bodleian Library in Oxford where he assisted in cataloguing the library's Chinese collection.

It is clear that Shen Fu-Tsung was heavily influenced by Father Philip Couplet. After leaving England in 1688, Shen Fu-Tsung himself became a Jesuit priest in Lisbon. Shen Fu-Tsung died near Mozambique, while travelling back to China in 1861.

John Anthony

The first Chinese to be a naturalised British citizen was John Anthony. John Anthony is believed to have arrived in Britain in the early 1790s. John Anthony converted to Christianity and was baptised at Saint Paul's Parish Church, Shadwell in 1799.

John Anthony, a native of Guangzhou Province, amassed a great fortune as the controller of Chinese and Indian seamen for the East India Company. It is almost certain that his wealth was gained through private trade, enjoyed by virtue of his position in the East India Company. He used at least part of this wealth to obtain British citizenship - an extremely costly affair as it required a private act of Parliament. His Bill of Naturalisation was passed in March 1805, though he was sadly not to enjoy his citizenship for very long, dying as he did in August of the same year, aged 39.

Married with children, the Anthony family had a country residence in Hallowall Down, Essex, (now Leytonstone, London). Reporting on hid funeral, The Gentleman's' Magazine reported:

The Bill of Naturalisation of John Anthony, August 1805.

"His body was removed to his residence in Shadwell, to be attended to that church by all the Chinese in town... He was carried to the grave in a hearse draw by six horses, preceded by four natives of China dressed in white, being the mourning of their country, with four lighted wax-tapers in their hands. Two mourning-coaches followed, with the friends of the deceased, and above 2000 of the neighbouring poor and other persons."

The Chinese Convert 1687
Sir Godfrey Kneller (1646 - 1723)
Royal Collection, Windsor

Chinese Influences

It is a little known fact that the Chinese made a significant contribution to Britain's war efforts during both the First and Second World Wars.

Almost 100,000 Chinese came to Europe during the Great War, not to fight, but rather to give logistical support to the British and French, freeing their soldiers from labouring tasks in order that they might engage in combat. Most notably the Chinese were contracted (as they were not fighting, they were not mercenaries) to perform the hard manual labour - perhaps the idea had come from the ability of the Chinese to build America's great railways where others had failed.

The Chinese were recruited in Shandong Province, and transported to France via the little known British colony of of Weihaiwai. Travel through Europe was not possible, and so the Chinese came via Canada - they could not initially use the Panama Canal because of US neutrality. Travelling conditions were atrocious – the men were transported across the whole of Canada in sealed trains as the Canadians feared they would "escape" and stay in Canada.

The Chinese Labour Corps worked in all manner of places, from ports to ordnance depots. They worked on the railways and roads and in digging the trenches. Many were employed in forestry, cutting down the trees to shore up the trenches on the western front or for building the huts which accommodated soldiers. Skilled Chinese workers were also employed as mechanics and builders.

Though the Chinese were not combatants, their work was dangerous, and conditions extremely poor. Two thousand died in service. At the largest Chinese war cemetery at Noyelles-sur-Mer in France, there are 870 graves. Their sacrifice is remembered with gratitude .

The Chinese Contribution to Peace in Europe

During the Second World War China was engaged in a fierce conflict with Japan. Nonetheless, the Chinese made an essential contribution to the British war effort. This time it came in the form of labourers for Allied shipping - mainly on the notorious transatlantic convoys. Around 20,000 Chinese sailors supported the Allied navy. Liverpool was their home base following the falls of Hong Kong (1941) and Singapore (1942).

Working on the transatlantic convoys was a perilous task, given that they were constantly targeted by the enemy. The Chinese had the manual jobs nobody else wanted to do, and where they were not seen – stoking the furnaces below decks. It was extremely hard work, with temperatures getting as high as 140 degrees Fahrenheit.

Once again– in Europe– the Chinese were not combatants, but their work was perilous. About 10% of all Chinese became casualties of the war, and there are numerous cases of Chinese having been held in Prisoner of War camps in Germany.

Like the Chinese in the Great War, their tasks were out of sight, and sadly have become out of mind. Though they did not operate the guns on the warships, the contribution of the Chinese to the war effort was vital.

Good Fellows

From the time the raw coolie arrived at the depot from his village in the interior of China until we deposited him in France, already half disciplined, I never ceased to admire his philosophic outlook on life; his sense of humour; his natural artistic bent; his generosity and his affection for his parents.

Just before sailing from China, we handed to each Coolie ten Mexican Dollars in Silver and gave him the option of leaving behind for his parents whatever portion of the ten dollars he cared to allot. In my company the average sum left behind for the parents at home was nine out of every ten dollars, a much greater proportion than would have been left behind for relatives by the privates of any British Regiment proceeding overseas on similar circumstances.

A small group of very dejected rejects passed in front of my Company which was on parade. On seeing them the Chief Coolie quickly asked my permission to make a collection for them. Soon his hat and the hats of several others were filled with coins, which they handed over to the rejects to cheer them up on their way to their village homes."

Excerpts from the memoirs of George E Cormack who accompanied 500 Chinese Labourers to France in 1917

Food is Essential

To the Chinese, food is a central aspect of their cultural inheritance. To illustrate this, one needs only to look at the history of 'food science' in China. It is generally agreed that the first systematic development of food hygiene and nutrition was developed by Lao Tzu – founder of Taoism– in the 6th century BC, and at roughly the same time Confucius developed the art of cooking. So it can be seen that there is a very strong link between food and the indigenous religions of China. Indeed, it was Confucius who taught that social ritual was a medium for teaching virtue, and consequently he who laid down the rules to be followed in recipes and the correct customs and etiquette to be observed at the table. As a result, traditional classical Chinese teaching promoted the belief that a true scholar not only mastered the arts of poetry, calligraphy, music and strategy, but also was a master of fine cuisine, which included food, wine and tea. To be a true scholar required mastering taste. As a result, a great wealth of material was written on food, taste and cooking.

The Chinese believe that the most important elements that help us appreciate taste are:

- colour
- aroma
- flavour
- texture

All of these elements must be combined to make a harmonious whole: it is the ability to create this harmony that the Chinese believe to be the art of cooking.

Interestingly, although the art of food appreciation is not really recognised in the West, the art of wine tasting is. Wine is judged on its bouquet (aroma), colour, flavour, and body- exactly the same attributes that were developed in China for appreciating food.

Colour

Colour is individual to each ingredient, and can change during cooking. At the same time the intensity of colour can change according to the colour of the other ingredients in the dish.

Aroma

Aroma and flavour are very closely related. The most common ingredients used in Chinese cooking to bring out the aroma of ingredients are spring onions, garlic, ginger and wine.

Flavour

Each school of cuisine has its own classification of flavours; however there are five primary flavours: sweet, sour, salty, bitter and piquant.

Texture

There are generally accepted to be five primary textures in Chinese cuisine: tenderness, crunchiness, crispiness, smoothness and softness. Very few Chinese dishes have only one ingredient, as this would offer no contrast and therefore no opportunity to harmonise and balance

Usually, there will be a main ingredient and a number of supplementary ingredients. Take pork for example. Its colour is pink and texture tender. It is most likely to be found with a green vegetable which is either crispy or crunchy such as celery (crunchy) or green peppers (crispy).

The concept of harmonisation doesn't stop with individual dishes, but is carried through the whole meal. No meal is made up of a single dish, but dishes are served in pairs, and often in fours. Similarly, the order in which food is served is dictated by the requirements of harmony. Monotony is to be avoided, and similar types of food are not served one after the other. From the individual dishes to the sequence of serving, the meal must be harmonious.

"Everyone eats and drinks, but few can appreciate taste".

Confucius

Customs relating to food

Dining etiquette, traditional eating habits, patterns, cuisine and diet are learned by all Chinese from an early age. Even the most modern of the younger generations tend to follow Chinese dining etiquette.

Meal time customs

Various customs relate to meal times at the Chinese table. Round dining tables are preferred to rectangular ones as they seat more people and allow diners to face each other without any implicit or explicit status differentiation in seating (such as the western tradition of the head of a household sitting at the 'head' of the table). At a meal, social status is levelled, and all are equal - well, that's the theory!

Mealtimes are the arena for family discussions, though the discussion of 'misfortunate' topics such as death is considered bad manners.

Other bad mannered practices include playing with the chopsticks during a meal (for example banging them on the table), or using a spoon used for personal eating for serving from a communal plate or bowl.

Tea

Tea

As in Britain, It is impossible to go anywhere in China without encountering people drinking tea. Tea is drunk all day -at work, at home, before and after meals, alone or in company. The absence of tea is an exception indeed rather than the rule in Chinese culture. China has an estimated 4 million acres given over to the growing of tea!

Tea drinking was invented by the Chinese, around the time of the Han dynasty (220 BC-200 AD), and many early Chinese tea customs gave rise to the elaborate tea ceremonies of other countries such as Japan. Drinking steeped leaf tea, however, emerged at the same time as fine white china during the Ming (1368-1644 AD) dynasty.

For all the myriad of tea available, there is only one tea plant (*Thea sinensis* or *Camellia sinensis* for the botanically minded). Variations in tea are accounted for by differences in the time of picking, rolling, fermentation and roasting. Broadly, there are three types of tea: unfermented green tea (prepared from fresh leaves and buds which are pan-fried then rolled and dried), semi-fermented tea such as Oolong (made by wilting the fresh leaves in the sun, then bruising them slightly and partially fermenting them) and fermented or 'black' tea (made by fermenting the slightly wilted leaves). The latter is the kind most often encountered in the West and India. In North China, green tea is often mixed with jasmine flowers to make a delicious and popular summertime drink.

Although Chinese in origin, tea is undoubtedly the national drink of Britain - a hot cup of tea being a cliched British response to any moment of crisis. Nothing is more British than a cup of tea - but then again, it can equally be said that nothing is more Chinese!

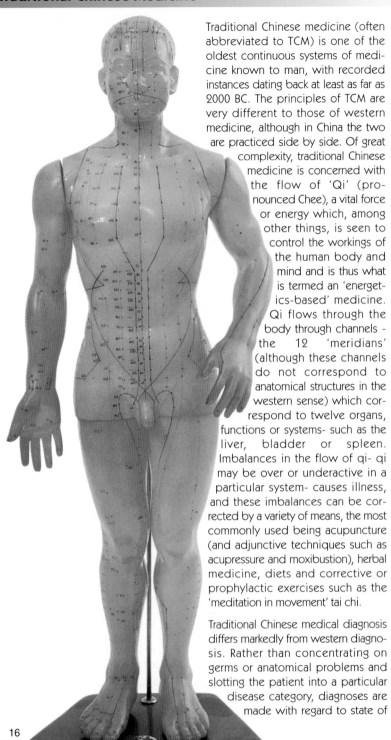

Traditional Chinese medicine (often abbreviated to TCM) is one of the oldest continuous systems of medicine known to man, with recorded instances dating back at least as far as 2000 BC. The principles of TCM are very different to those of western medicine, although in China the two are practiced side by side. Of great complexity, traditional Chinese medicine is concerned with the flow of 'Qi' (pronounced Chee), a vital force or energy which, among other things, is seen to control the workings of the human body and mind and is thus what is termed an 'energetics-based' medicine. Qi flows through the body through channels - the 12 'meridians' (although these channels do not correspond to anatomical structures in the western sense) which correspond to twelve organs, functions or systems- such as the liver, bladder or spleen. Imbalances in the flow of qi- qi may be over or underactive in a particular system- causes illness, and these imbalances can be corrected by a variety of means, the most commonly used being acupuncture (and adjunctive techniques such as acupressure and moxibustion), herbal medicine, diets and corrective or prophylactic exercises such as the 'meditation in movement' tai chi.

Traditional Chinese medical diagnosis differs markedly from western diagnosis. Rather than concentrating on germs or anatomical problems and slotting the patient into a particular disease category, diagnoses are made with regard to state of the qi. Although there are many and complex ways of diagnosing in TCM, the most important are through the pulse (where the energy of the meridians is assessed by the strength, rhythm and quality of the pulse), the tongue's colour, quality etc. and the general appearance, demeanour etc. of the person. Thus a patient with what western medicine would diagnose as having a particular skin disease for example, may be seen as having 'excess heat in the liver', another who would have the same problem to western doctors may have 'damp spleen'. Although the principles of traditional Chinese medicine may look very exotic or even esoteric to western eyes, the effectiveness of much TCM has been demonstrated by many scientific experiments. In practice, it is often used on a more pragmatic rather than philosophical basis- that is, if it works, use it! As well as some widely reported recent successes in trials and practices for the treatment of skin disorders, many western doctors also practice acupuncture and in the 1990s the first Chinese herbal medicine clinic in a National Health Service hospital opened in London.

Acupuncture

The best-known technique of traditional Chinese medicine, acupuncture consists of the insertion of extremely fine needles through the skin. The needles are inserted at particular points along the paths of the meridians in order to balance the qi and stimulate healing.

At a usual acupuncture session between two and six needles are inserted through the skin. They may be rotated slightly, and left in place for a period of about half an hour. Because the needles used in acupuncture are extremely fine, they do not cause pain in the same way as, say, an injection or pricking one's finger with a pin: often there may be no feeling at all, a slight tickling or tingling or sometimes a slight pain.

Some practitioners use a process known as 'moxibustion', where a special herb or 'moxa'- usually in the form of a cone of dried herb- is burned on, or just above, the surface of the skin (though removed before the skin can be burned!) at the acupuncture 'points'. This has a warming and nourishing effect on the qi.

Some therapists practice what is know as 'acupressure', which is stimulation of the acupuncture points by pressing with the fingers.

Initial responses to an acupuncture session may vary- often a patient may feel pleasantly drowsy, or sometimes elated or 'high'.

An acupuncturist may also prescribe herbal remedies, and give dietary and other lifestyle advice.

Acupuncture can be used for many conditions, and is especially well suited to the treatment and /or management of pain, both acute and chronic.

Even though it involves the insertion of needles, acupuncture in skilled hands is a very safe therapy. Worldwide the number of cases of problems occurring because of acupuncture is minuscule, and problems usually occur when acupuncture is practiced by the poorly trained or untrained.

All reputable acupuncturists will either use fresh 'virgin' needles for each new patient, or sterilise needles before reuse to avoid the possibility of infection.

Chinese Herbal Medicine

Chinese herbal medicine has received much publicity over recent years, particularly with regard to some sometimes spectacular cures of skin diseases.

Just as an acupuncturist uses the insertion of needles to correct imbalances in the flow of qi, so a herbalist will prescribe herbs.

Chinese herbal medicine is a very ancient form of medicine, with the oldest Chinese book about herbs, the Shen Nong Ben Cao credited to the legendary Emperor Shennong, who is thought to have lived around 2700 BC.

There are six thousand herbs currently used in Chinese herbal medicine, and from these countless formulas are devised for use with patients. There are some standard formulas, but each patient will also be given a unique formula to match his/her unique state of ill health and his/her constitution

Although the vast majority of 'herbs' used in Chinese herbal medicine are plants, some animal/insect materials— such as lizard, centipede and scorpion— and minerals are occasionally used (though not very frequently in the UK!). The distinction between herbs and food can become quite blurred in TCM, and dietary advice alongside a prescription is very likely when visiting a Chinese herbalist.

Chinese herbalists diagnose using the same methods and principles as acupuncturists and after a diagnosis is reached, the patient will be prescribed a mixture of herbs, usually dried, to be taken in the form of a 'decoction', that is boiled in water, though sometimes powders, ointments, tablets and tinctures (alcohol-based preparations) may be used. One thing that most western patients agree on is that Chinese herbal preparations are not always very pleasant tasting- they can, however be very effective. Chinese herbal medicine, depending on the problem and person being treated, can have quite rapid and spectacular results, but more often there isa gradual, steady progression towards health is seen.

Properly used or prescribed, Chinese herbal medicine is a safe form of treatment, and compared to Western orthodox drugs, Chinese herbs are for the most part relatively non-toxic in nature, as well as causing fewer or no side effects. Poisonings occasionally occur- usually accompanied by a great deal of hysterical press coverage- but these are almost always from a patient not following the instructions of his / her herbalist, or from ill-informed self prescription.

Medicinal uses of tea

In herbal medicine the different types of tea have certain medicinal properties.

Green tea contains a high amount of fluoride which may help reduce tooth decay- it was commonly used for centuries by Chinese peasants for cleaning the teeth. Green tea can also be used externally to stop or slow bleeding from cuts and scrapes and to relieve itchy insect bites. Some varieties of oolong tea have cholesterol-lowering properties which are especially effective if the tea is drunk after a fatty meal.

Oolong tea may also reduce blood pressure and arterial disease, possibly by decreasing the clotting tendency of blood.

Black tea is rich in chemicals called tannins which are astringent. For herbalists these are useful in treating diarrhoea. Cooled, damp black tea bags may also be placed over tired, red eyes or on insect bites to relieve redness and itching.

Finding a TCM Practitioner

Although a number of shops selling Chinese herbs have appeared in the UK in recent years, most people prefer to visit a practitioner of traditional Chinese medicine when undertaking TCM treatment. Finding a good practitioner of TCM is not always easy, and is sometimes a case of 'hit and miss'. In the UK there are no regulations governing the practice of TCM: in theory, anyone- with little or no training- can set up in practice as an 'acupuncturist' or 'Chinese herbalist'. Similarly, anyone can set up a 'School of Chinese Medicine' and give out certificates, or start up a register of TCM practitioners with an impressive sounding name.

The very best guide to finding a good acupuncturist or Chinese herbalist is by word of mouth or reputation. Perhaps a friend, relative or neighbour has been successfully treated and can recommend a practitioner. If your doctor is one of the growing number who recognise the value of non-Western medicines, he or she may know of or be able to suggest a good local practitioner.

If you cannot find a practitioner by personal recommendation, the local press or Yellow Pages or other directories may list practitioners. There may also be professional associations of Chinese medical practitioners who may be able to recommend a practitioner in your area. Do not feel afraid to ask a practitioner about his or her qualifications or experience before making an appointment to see them (most practitioners will work on an appointment system). Practitioners trained in China itself have often received some of the best TCM training.

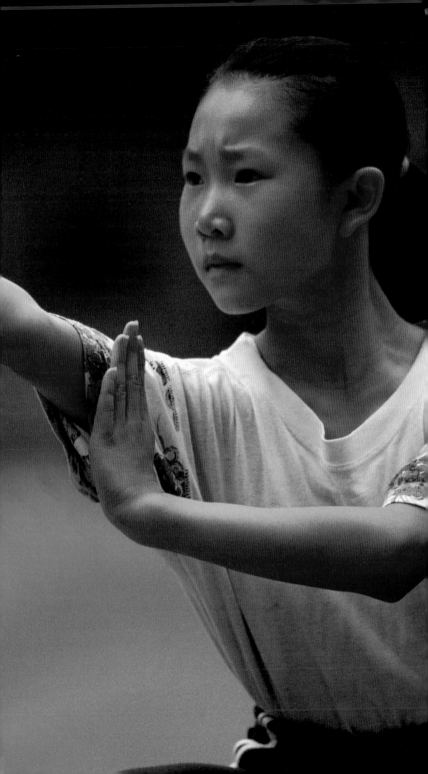

Kung Fu

In the 70s Chinese *kung fu* became a craze across Western Europe and North America, and for the first time Chinese films found a mass audience in these places.

Like many cultural concepts from China, kung fu was largely presented in a simplistic way, and became associated with extreme violence. In many ways this shouldn't be a great surprise, as most people's experience of 'kung fu' is either from films or video games. However, a closer look at martial arts will show that this is in fact far from the truth. Fundamental to all Chinese martial arts are the concepts of respect, self-discipline, courtesy and inner strength, and the use of the arts for offensive purposes goes against these fundamental principles.

Chinese 'kung fu' is a misnomer. Kung fu means 'great skill', and somewhere this was taken to be the name of what the Chinese call Wushu - martial arts. Wushu originated in the famous Shaolin Temple of Henan Province. It took about 20 years of rigorous training for a trainee monk to become a true Shaolin monk. As time went on the monks of Shaolin became legendary figures who would fight on the side of good against evil. The temple was at its height of power during the Tang dynasty (7-10th centuries AD). In the Ming dynasty (14-17th centuries AD) weapons were added to some disciplines, and over the centuries a number of distinct forms have emerged.

Yin and Yang

The practice of martial arts, like so many aspects of Chinese culture, is strongly linked with the concepts of "*Yin and Yang*". Yin and yang represent the idea of harmony and balance.

Often described as positive and negative, yin and yang is a little more subtle than this, with the idea being that the world is in a state of balance. For example, there are males and females. Together they create the balanced state of the world. In some situations there will be more males than females, which will have a localised effect: at the global level the balance is maintained. Local imbalances can have detrimental effects in the long term, and so there is a constant thriving to maintain balance. Where man intervenes to such an extent as to destabilise the global balance, then remedies become much more problematic.

The Tai Chi Symbol, often referred to as the Yin Yang symbol

Tai Chi

Tai chi is a very ancient form of gentle movement exercise, that has its origin many thousands of years ago. In many ways it straddles the boundaries between martial arts, exercise and meditation, and can be practiced solo, or by two people, the so-called 'pushing hands' technique.

There are many forms of tai chi, though all consist of exercises practiced following a very precise pattern, which is usually learned and refined in concert with a tai chi teacher. There is also a form of tai chi known as 'qi gong' in which special breathing techniques are co-ordinated with movement.

Tai chi is very graceful- both to watch and to perform, and is based on Taoist philosophies, that is, life is lived most effectively if a person refrains from fighting against the natural ebb and flow of yin and yang. Each movement in tai chi 'created' naturally by its predecessor, thus minimising effort and creating a flowing, liquid exercise.

Although some forms of tai chi can be and are taught as self defence, it is a martial art only in that it creates

health and well-being through enhanced balance, strength and concentration: it is not the intent of tai chi to put these to violent uses. Rather, tai chi is performed for personal development and pleasure.

Because it is a very gentle form of exercise, tai chi is suitable for just about everyone (there is even a seated variant for those who may be wheelchair bound), and can be of great benefit for physical health problems- such as arthritis or for aiding recovery after disease- as well as being an excellent way of removing the effects of stress. It thus has a wide applicability in the hectic modern world.

Tai chi classes are very commonplace in adult education centres, sports centres and other venues.

Qi Gong

Qi gong roughly translates as 'bio-energy exercise'. This isn't a literal translation, but rather a paraphrase as there is no English word for 'qi' in this context. Ordinarily it can mean breath, and perhaps this begins to give an insight into the life-holding proper-ties of qi. The qiof qi gong has been described as 'vital energy' or 'life force', and it is the basis on which Chinese tradition-al medicine is founded. If qi is considered to be your bio-energy, then qi gong is essen-tially exercises to ensure that your qi remains in a stable, balanced state. Imbalance will cause illness, and so the connection with health is clear.

Qi gong dates back five thou-sand years and is intended for improving and maintaining health as well as to help cure disease. The basic aim is to bring the body into a state of balance and self-regula-tion.

Qi gong has been the subject of intense scientific research in China in recent years, and there is consider-able evidence that the art does have beneficial effects on health. Rather like acupuncture, nobody is quite sure why. It has been suggested that qi gong has the effect of 'super-oxy-genating' cells, and this in turn leads to beneficial health effects'.

Whether or not science is able to demonstrate the cause and effects of qi gong, there is ample evidence that demonstrates that something extra-ordinary is going on, and masters of qi gong can demonstrate great feats of strength and endurance. The most famous demonstration of qi gong is the smashing of bricks with a 'karate chop'. Other demonstra-tions include the breaking of pig iron bars by smashing them on the head and the withstanding of spears against flesh (these practices are extremely dangerous, and should not be tried at home).

Most practitioners of qi gong do not take the art to this level, but rather see it as a means of promoting good health. Quite often qi gong practitioners can be seen exercis-ing in the early morn-ing alongside practition-ers of tai qi - indeed, it is common to practice both.

Excessive practice of qi gong has been linked with negative side effects. As in so many things, excess is not recommended, and indeed, should be avoided.

Wing Chun

Wing Chun is arguably the style of martial arts that most people think about when they hear the words 'kung fu'. It originated in the Shaolin temple, and was popularised by Bruce Lee, although Bruce Lee had his own particular style of Wing Chun. The Wing Chun style is one of the most popular 'fighting styles' in the West.

Wing Chun, on the face of it, is a fairly basic form of martial arts, and some have misunderstood this to mean it is rudimentary. However, the simplicity is a result of extreme refinement, and as such it is a highly developed art.

Wing Chun's origins, like so many forms of martial arts, are lost in legend and myth, and several stories of the origin of Wing Chun exist. All agree that the form was created by a Shaolin 'nun' called Ng Mui, a senior kung fu practitioner who was interested in combining the best techniques from the broad array of traditional Shaolin kung fu into a simple, master style. It is said that the techniques were developed when Ng Mui observed a battle between a crane and a snake.

Ng Mui met a young woman named Wing Chun (Beautiful Springtime) who was being forced to marry a local warlord who had threatened to kill her and her father if she did not. Wing Chun, on the guidance of Ng Mui got a delay of one year before the marriage, during which time Ng Mui passed on her art to Wing Chun. On the day of the wedding, Wing Chun challenged the warlord to a duel, and humiliated him. In this way she and her family were freed from tyranny, and the Wing Chun style was born.

Guan Di, the Chinese God of War. Guan Di is the mightiest of all Chinese gods, and is seen as a protector.

Guan Di

Guan Di, who is also known as Guan Gung, is commonly referred to in the West as the Chinese "god of war". However, this is a bit of a misnomer, as in fact Guan Di is a protector, and so in that respect is the god that protects against war. A more appropriate title would be the "god who defends the state, civilisation and morality".

Guan Di is regarded as the patron god of the Qing dynasty, the military, the police, of restaurants, pawn shops, curio-dealers of some aspects of wealth, and of literature.

In fact Guan Di lived from 162 to 220AD. He was a famous warrior, and his tales are told in the Chinese classical novel *The Romance of the Three Kingdoms*. Guan Di's characteristic red face has several myths attached to it, but perhaps the most endearing (if not the most probable) is the story that he is red in the face through righteous indignation.

As the most powerful of all the Chinese gods, Guan Di is to be found in many homes, where his statue or image faces the front door, dispelling any evil as evil spirits will flee merely on the sight of his face.

One tale associated with Guan Di tells of a travelling theatrical company who are approached by a stranger and commissioned to perform in a great mansion, and for which they will be paid handsomely. The one condition is that none of the plays performed should include the character of Guan Di.

The performers arrive at the great house, which is so magnificent that the actors are quite taken aback. Convinced that they are going to be well paid, the actors perform for a crowd who seems very appreciative of the performances.

However, as time goes on, the actors become less and less impressed, as they are offered no refreshments whatsoever. As the night goes on they become more and more put out by this lack of consideration, and therefore plot to make a protest to their clients. Mindful of the instruction that Guan Di must not appear in any of the performances, the actors decide to perform a piece in which Guan Di is the main character.

As Guan Di comes onto the stage there is sudden gasp from the audience, and then, in the blinking of an eye everyone in the audience disappears. The actors find themselves in a the grounds of an abandoned mansion, with an overgrown garden. Only then do they realise that they have been performing for a party of ghosts.

Learn
Chinese

萬里之外，學習
中國語言文化

- Fully accredited
- Learn at your own pace
- Credit based learning
- Study up to degree level
- Internationally recognised University
- Summer schools in Beijing, China
- No long term commitment
- Flexible, pay-as-you-learn
- Full online tutorial support

北京語言文化大學

Feng Shui

Feng shui has its origins in Taoism, and is the art of living in harmony with the environment.

'Feng' is the Chinese word for wind, and 'shui' the word for water. These are the two elements which form our environment, both through the creation of the landscape, and also in the weather.

The precise roots of feng shui are shrouded in legend. It is widely believed that the origins of the art lay in the writing of Fu Xi. Fu Xi is sometimes referred to as a scholar, and sometimes as one of China's earliest Emperors.

Legend has it that one day Fu Xi was deep in thought standing on the banks of a river when he observed a turtle emerging from out of the flowing waters. The turtle was famed for its longevity, and was regarded as a sacred animal. Fu Xi noticed strange markings on the turtle's back, and so copied them into the river bank's sand, later putting them into a book, which became known as the He Shu (River Book). This was later developed

into the I Ching (Book of Changes), from which feng shui originates.

Feng shui practitioners believe that everything is made of qi or energy which is organised into five elements: metal, fire, water, wood and earth. Each element has associated seasons, colours, directions, shapes and so on. The degree to which these elements dominate or are absent has a resulting effect upon the environment, and the balance of qi.

Once, practicing feng shui was punishable by death as it was an art that was strictly restricted to China's Imperial household. Today feng shui is widely practiced by Chinese in communities across the globe, and in recent years has become increasingly popular in North America, Europe, Australia and New Zealand.

Bronze turtle in Beijing's Forbidden City.

Colours

Colours have particular significance in feng shui, either generating qi energy or dampening it. Even those who do not follow feng shui will agree that colours can have a dramatic effect on the ambience of a place: feng shui suggests that choosing the right colour can have a great impact on personal happiness and success.

Reds

Red is the colour of life, is vibrant and energetic and has associations with passion. It is considered so powerful by the Chinese as to even be able to ward off evil.

Yellows

Sometimes an arresting colour, yellow is associated with soil, and promotes thought and freshness.

Greens

Green is strongly linked to the wood element which brings warmth and life. Therefore greens stimulates growth and vitality.

Blues

Blue has strong associations with harmony, and is linked to both loyalty and trustworthiness.

Purples

Purple is often associated with philosophers, and accordingly it is linked to wisdom and truth. It is a strong colour and can be associated with passion.

The Five Elements

Central to feng shui are the five elements. The translation of the Chinese word 'xing' as elements is in some ways inappropriate, though it is probably the closest English equivalent. The elements are in fact states of being which can change from one form to another. It is clear that as these forms change, then they must change from one element to another. In feng shui there are 'productive' and 'destructive' cycles.

The Productive Cycle

Fire $\xrightarrow{\text{Produces}}$ Water $\xrightarrow{\text{Produces}}$ Wood $\xrightarrow{\text{Produces}}$ Metal $\xrightarrow{\text{Produces}}$ Earth $\xrightarrow{\text{Produces}}$

Fire	Water	Wood	Metal	Earth
Associated with expansion, energy, light, summer, the south and red.	Associated with irregular shapes, winter, the north and blue.	Associated with growth, power, spring, the east and green	Associated with maturity, autumn, the west and orange	Associated with stability, safety, the centre and yellow

The Destructive Cycle

Fire $\xrightarrow{\text{Destroys}}$ Metal $\xrightarrow{\text{Destroys}}$ Wood $\xrightarrow{\text{Destroys}}$ Earth $\xrightarrow{\text{Destroys}}$ Water $\xrightarrow{\text{Destroys}}$

The Eight Trigrams

Fundamental to feng shui are the Eight Trigrams, or Ba Gua. These eight symbols comprise of a combination of solid (yang) or broken (yin) lines. There are eight possible ways to combine these two sets of lines, and these eight combinations make the Ba Gua.

The Ba Gua Mirror

These are used as a guard against evil, and it is common to see them above doors that face in a bad direction.

The effect of the Ba Gua mirror is to repel the bad qi energy by reflecting it back from where it came. The power is not in the mirror, this is a symbolic aspect, but rather in the trigrams decorating the frame.

Worlds First Computer!

Developed over 5000 years ago, the solid and broken lines which make up the trigrams are believed to be the earliest use of a binary system, the system on which all computers and digital information is based on today.

A Feng Shui Compass

Chinese New Year

China's Biggest Festival

The oldest and most important festival in China is the Spring Festival, more commonly known in the West as Chinese New Year. Like all traditional Chinese festivals, the date of the new year is determined by the Chinese lunar-solar calendar rather than the Western solar calendar, so the date of the holiday varies from late January to early February.

The Spring festival celebrates the earth coming back to life, and the start of ploughing and sowing. In the past, feudal rulers of dynasties placed great importance on this occasion, and ceremonies to usher in the season were performed.

Preparations for the New Year festival start during the last few days of the last moon. Houses are thoroughly

cleaned, debts repaid, hair cut and new clothes bought. Doors are decorated with vertical scrolls of characters on red paper whose texts seek good luck and praise nature, this practice stemming from the hanging of peachwood charms to keep away ghosts and evil spirits. In many homes incense is burned, and also in the temples as a mark of respect to ancestors.

On New Year's Eve houses are brightly lit and a large family dinner is served. In the south of China sticky-sweet glutinous rice pudding called *nian gao* is served, while in the north the steamed dumpling *jiaozi* is popular. Most celebrating the festival stay up till midnight, when fireworks are lit, to drive away evil spirits. New Year's day is often spent visiting neighbours, family and friends.

The public holiday for New Year lasts three days in China, but the festival traditionally lasts till the 15th day of the lunar month and ends with the 'Lantern Festival'. Here, houses are decorated with colourful lanterns, and *yuanxioa*, a sweet or savoury fried or boiled dumpling made of glutinous rice flour is eaten.

The Lion Dance

The most spectacular event of the Chinese New Year festivities must surely be the Lion Dance. Lion dances take place throughout the first few days of the Chinese New Year, and bring good luck to the households or businesses which they visit. The Lion Dance itself is performed by two 'dancers' one at the head and one at the tail of the lion. Careful observation of the Lion Dance will show that it is in fact a very careful demonstration of stylised movements performed by skilled performers (generally from a martial arts school or acrobatic company). To enhance the 'life' of the lion, the eyelids, mouth and ears of the Lion's head all move. The dance is accompanied by loud music played on large drum, gong and cymbals. The use of firecrackers, drums, gongs and cymbals are related to the role of the lion in dispelling evil and bringing good luck - evil being afraid of loud noise

The dramatic climax of the Lion Dance is the *Choi Cheng* or 'picking the green'. The green here refers to vegetable leaves which are tied to a piece of string which also has a red packet attached containing money. The string is hung above the door of the house or business, and the lion 'eats' both leaves and red packet. Lying on the floor the leaves are 'chewed' by the lion while the musicians play a dramatic rolling crescendo. The lull is broken as the lion explodes back into activity while spitting out the leaves. This is a symbolic act of blessing by the lion, with the spitting out of the leaves signifying that there will be an abundance of everything in the coming year.

Nian

The New Year Monster is Nian. In Chinese *nian* simply means 'year'. However, it is widely accepted that the origin of this word comes from the mythical monster that would come and terrorise humans around the time of the New Year. Indeed, so fierce was Nian that it threatened to destroy mankind. The Emperor summoned a wise man to solve this problem. Seeing at first hand the destruction Nian brought, the wise man approached Nian with a challenge. "Why do you choose to kill and destroy the humans who are no match for your strength?" he asked. "Prove your real power by destroying the other monsters of the earth." Nian took up this challenge, and one year later, having destroyed all the monsters of the earth, he returned to terrorise

The Chinese dragon brings good luck, and dispels evil

mankind. However, the very day he returned some children were playing with firecrackers, and they noticed that Nian was afraid of the noise. From then on each New Year firecrackers and other fireworks are used to scare away the last monster on earth– Nian.

New Year Taboos

Avoid housework on New Year's day: this activity runs the risk of washing or sweeping away good luck. For the same reason, avoid washing your hair on the first and last day of the New Year. It is also considered unlucky to use anything sharp on New Year's day - knives, scissors, even nail clippers. The action of the sharp blades risks cutting the threads of good fortune brought in at New Year. It is important not to use language which is negative- having an argument on New Year's day is to be avoided at all costs. Words related to sickness and death are to be avoided, and even words which *sound* like words related to sickness or death. To avoid any association with death, any slaughtering of poultry or livestock is carried out on New Year's Eve. Finally, care must be taken not to stumble or to break anything - this would be indicative of bad luck ahead.

Chinese Festival Dates 2002 - 2004

Chinese New Year
The first day of the first lunar month.

2003	1 February
2004	22 January
2005	9 February

Lantern Festival
The fifteenth day of the first lunar month.

2003	15 February
2004	5 February
2005	23 February

Dragon Boat Festival
The fifth day of the fifth lunar month.

2003	4 June
2004	22 June
2005	11 June

Moon Festival
The fifteenth day of the eighth lunar month.

2003	11 September
2004	28 September
2005	18 September

Red Couplets

Decorations are an important feature of the celebrations for the Chinese New Year. One of the main forms of decoration are the 'Red Couplets', which are Chinese good luck sayings written on red paper, often with gold trimmings and usually made up of four Chinese characters which ask for luck in terms of long life, wealth etc.

Red is not only a lucky colour for the Chinese, but also frightens off the monster Nian who arrives at this time of year and destroys crops and homes. Some New Year couplets are intended to be pasted or pinned in special places such as the kitchen or doors, while some can be placed anywhere. The couplets are usually taken down after the New Year celebrations, though some people keep them up all year long in the hope of keeping good luck.

Red Packets

Red packets are every child's delight at Chinese New Year! The tradition of giving gifts in Chinese culture is not the same as practiced in British culture. By and large the giving of gifts is restricted to giving money. Small gifts are given when visiting the home of a friend, and increasingly for weddings, but traditionally money is given. The way in which this is done in the Britain would be by putting money in a card, or indeed, giving a gift voucher. The Chinese give money inside red envelopes which are decorated with lucky symbols or Chinese characters. These are known as 'Lai Si' or 'Hung Bao'. At Chinese New Year these are given by married couples to children or unmarried people. Red is used as the most auspicious colour, while the decoration may have a blessing or good wish. The symbolic giving of the money represents a wish for fortune and wealth in the coming year. The money may also be used to pay off debt, thus allowing a financial clean slate in the new year.

Fortune Sticks

The New Year is obviously a time when people are mindful of the future. Often people will have their fortunes told at the temple. The oldest known method of fortune telling in the world is known as Kau Chime – a set of 78 numbered sticks held in a bamboo case. Holding the container in both hands and shaking it causes one of the sticks to rise and fall out. The number on the stick is matched with a numbered ancient texts, and a fortune told. The fortune is generally a short poem or rhyme, and the point is not so much to have a clear prediction, but an indication of the possibilities which lie ahead.

The Chinese are not, by and large, fatalistic, though they hold many superstitious beliefs. Therefore, having one's fortune told is more an indication of the conditions ahead rather than actual events. The opportunity therefore exists for people to make the most of their lives by being more aware of the 'environmental conditions' which surround their lives. If you don't like what the fortune teller says, you do something about it!

Kitchen God's Day

On the 24th day of the last lunar month the kitchen god returns to heaven to give a report to the Jade Emperor (the ruler of heaven) about the family's activities over the past year. This day is marked by acts of appeasement to the kitchen god so that he will give the Jade Emperor a favourable report. Traditionally images of the kitchen god are burned as a symbolic act of departure. Often some gold or silver money will also be burned for travelling expenses. In some households the lips of the kitchen god are brushed with honey just before the image is burned – this will increase the likelihood that only sweet things will be said by the kitchen god. From the 24th the Kitchen god will be absent from his shrine in the kitchen, and during this time it will be cleaned in preparation for his return on New Year's Eve.

Traditional New Year painting showing children (representing happiness and security) playing with firecrackers, carrying great wealth and the "Gung Hei Fat Choi" banner on a staff representing long life. The character on the lantern is "Chun" meaning Spring.

Flowers

Flowers hold a special significance at Chinese New Year, and the Chinese language's endless opportunities for puns and play on words are demonstrated in the flowers which are used. As with almost all activities at Chinese New Year, there is enormous symbolism in the use of flowers.

In Chinese cities around the world, flower fairs appear on the 26th day of the last moon, and run each evening until New Year's Eve. A stroll through the flower fair is a New Year ritual many Chinese enjoy, even after they've got all their flowers; indeed, it's a popular way of spending New Year's Eve while waiting to see in the New Year. Three of the most significant flowers are:

Blossoms

Blossoms are particularly auspicious flowers. Coming as they do in spring they symbolise life, growth and prosperity. The peach blossom is the most auspicious of all plants, its significance lying in the symbolic importance of the peach. The peach, in Chinese culture, is a symbol of long life, and is regarded as the strongest defence against evil. Should your peach blossom bloom during the New Year celebrations it is sure sign that the year ahead will be one of good fortune. Sprays of peach blossom at one time were placed above front doors to prevent even the strongest evil spirit from getting into the house. The custom today is to use them as decorations within the house.

Peony

In Chinese the peony is called the 'Flower of Riches and Honour', and is the emblem of love and affection,

as well as being a symbol for feminine beauty. The bright red peony is particularly auspicious, bringing with it luck and good fortune.

Kumquat Tree

Kumquat is a play on Chinese words. In Chinese the kumquat is called Gam Gat Sue. The word Gam rhymes with the Chinese word for gold, and the word Gat rhymes with the Chinese word for luck. Therefore the name sounds like "Gold and Luck". In addition, the tiny green leaves of this plant symbolise wealth as the word Luk (green) rhymes with the Chinese word for wealth. Finally the shape of the small oranges are a symbol of unity and perfection.

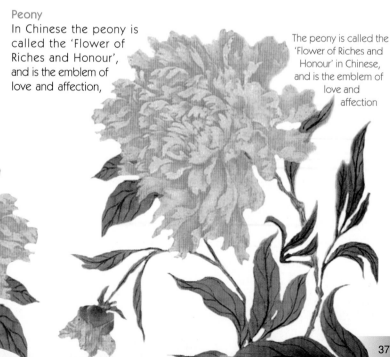

The peony is called the 'Flower of Riches and Honour' in Chinese, and is the emblem of love and affection

The Twelve Animals

The origins of the twelve animals which are honoured with a year each is rich in legends and myths. The most popular legend says that Buddha decided to invite all the animals of the earth to visit him on New Year's Day. However, despite preparing for the biggest party since the disembarkation of Noah's Ark, only twelve animals arrived. They were the Rat, the Ox, the Tiger, the Rabbit, the Dragon, the Snake, the Horse, the Ram, the Monkey, the Rooster, the Dog and the Pig. Buddha decided to honour his guests by awarding each a year of its own, with the order being the same order as they had arrived. It is said that the rat, or mouse (which are called the same thing in Chinese) was determined to be the first, and feared the speed of the cat. The cat was tricked by the rat into being a day late : that is why the cat and the mouse are eternal enemies.

1924 1936 1948 1960 1972 1984 1996	**The Rat** Generous, intelligent and polite. Often private and reserved.	1930 1942 1954 1966 1978 1990 2002	**The Horse** Loyal, eloquent and enigmatic. Shines in social situations.
1925 1937 1949 1961 1973 1985 1997	**The Ox** Honest, placid and considerate. Thinks things through.	1931 1943 1955 1967 1979 1991 2003	**The Ram** Gentle, amiable and peaceful. Enjoys the finer things in life.
1926 1938 1950 1962 1974 1986 1998	**The Tiger** Competitive, optimistic and a good leader. Loves a challenge.	1932 1944 1956 1968 1980 1992 2004	**The Monkey** Independent, sociable and perceptive. Can be mischievous.
1927 1939 1951 1963 1975 1987 1999	**The Rabbit** Tranquil, sensitive and generous. A natural peacemaker.	1933 1945 1957 1969 1981 1993 2005	**The Rooster** Courageous, open and indulgent. Will always help those in need.
1928 1940 1952 1964 1976 1988 2000	**The Dragon** Energetic, impressive and dynamic. Always ready with ideas.	1934 1946 1958 1970 1982 1994 2006	**The Dog** Loyal, observant and trustworthy. Sensitive to situations.
1929 1941 1953 1965 1977 1989 2001	**The Snake** Refined, elegant and polite. A great debater.	1935 1947 1959 1971 1983 1995 2007	**The Pig** Calm, tolerant and private. Mixes well with others.

英文
词

Some words are obviously Chinese, and the reason we have them in the English language is because there is no equivalent in English, so they have been adopted. These include cheongsam (a Chinese dress) kung fu, tai chi, chop suey, chow mein and sampan - a type of boat. But there are other words which are less obviously Chinese, and which often have interesting stories behind them. Here are some of them.

Ketchup

The word ketchup was derived from "ke-tsiap" in the Fukienese dialect, and was the word for a particular type of sauce. The name and perhaps some samples arrived in England where it appeared in print as "catchup" in 1690 and then as "ketchup" in 1711. It was a generic term for a variety of sauces, but eventually became associated with one - tomato sauce.

Tea

Tea is also known as Cha, and this is both the Mandarin and Cantonese word for tea. It may seem strange then that the commonest word is completely different. The reason lies in China's many dialects. 'Tea' is

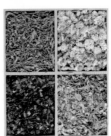

derived, like 'ketchup', from the Fukienese. Fukien was formerly called Amoy, Amoy being one of the earliest trading points with the Western world in China. In the Fukienese dialect, tea is 'de', and was mispronounce as 'tea'.

Kowtow

To act obsequiously. This comes directly from the Mandarin Ketou, which literally translates as "to knock the head". This refers to the practice of falling prostrate before the Emperor and hitting the head against the floor.

Silk

As the Chinese discovered silk, it is hardly surprising that the word in English comes from Chinese. It is directly related to the Chinese word "Si" (pronounced as "see") for silk.

Gungho

Eager or spirited. It is derived from "Gung He" which is the abbreviated form of the term "Gung zuo he zuo she" which loosely translated means "Working Together Society". Gung Ho literally translates as "Working together". It was the spirit of the Chinese in working towards a common goal, particularly against great adversity, that so impressed the US Marines during the Second World War, that they adopted it as their motto - and the word entered the English language.

Chow

Food. This word for food is derived from the Mandarin word "Jiao", meaning a dumpling, a staple food during the winter months in northern China. From this we get derived words such as chowhound, chow line and chowtime.

Tofu

Beancurd. Tofu is a word which has been corrupted through its introduction into English from Chinese by a third language, Japanese. Tofu originates from the Chinese 'daofu', but came came via Japanese where it was pronounced tofu.

Shanghai

To forcibly abduct someone into service. It originates from the practice of ship's captains in San Fransisco who would get sailors drunk and then make them sign up for the voyages to Shanghai.

Chopsticks

It is not immediately evident why chopsticks are so-called. Clearly they are sticks, but they do not chop. The chop part of the word is the same as is used in the phrase "chop-chop" meaning quickly, or hurry-up. This is derived from the Cantonese word "Kap" meaning quick. So Chopsticks actually means "fast-sticks" which makes no more sense than "chopsticks" except when it is explained that in Chinese, chopsticks are called "quai-zi" which can roughly be translated as "fast ones".

Typhoon

This is a direct transliteration of the Cantonese Tai-fung, which simply means "Great Wind".

Kaolin

A clay used in fine porcelain production, as well as medicinal uses. Kaolin is a mispronunciation of the word 'Gaoling', the name of a hill in China where the clay was mined. Part of the reason for the corruption in pronunciation is that it came to English via French.

Yen

A craving or longing. The word 'yen' comes from the Cantonese word 'yan' which describes the craving of a drug addict for a drug, particularly used to describe opium users (see historical context, page 10). The connotation with drug craving has long been lost.

Chin Chin

Chin chin can mean hello or goodbye, and once a popular toast, it is derived from the Mandarin (qing) or in Cantonese (ching) which means 'please'. Repetition of words in Chinese is used for emphasis – so 'qing qing' would be a greeting or welcome to a home.

Shopping

Enter Chinatown and a whole new world of products suddenly become available. What seems everyday and ordinary to the Chinese can seem curious if not outright baffling to non-Chinese.

This section begins to introduce some common Chinese products which can be found in every Chinatown across Britain. Hopefully it will give you the confidence to try some new things.

It's obviously impossible to create an exhaustive list of the products on sale in Chinatown, but should you see something which you want to know more about, then ask. The store keeper will, if they can, explain what it is. Should you receive a puzzled look in response, don't be put off: this is more likely to be due to the difficulty of explaining some things which, quite simply, may have no English equivalent.

All that aside, in restaurants you can always point and give it a go - even more so in the ever popular Chinese bakeries.

Although not covered in this section, all of Britain's Chinatowns have bookshops and arts and crafts stores as well as music shops – wander in and have a browse. Some books are in English, and as for the music, well you may come out a new fan of Cantopop (Cantonese pop music) or hooked on Chinese traditional music. Shop till you drop, and then go for dim sum as a well earned reward!

Happy shopping!

- Ordering Dim Sum

- Menu Converter

- At the Chinese
  Supermarket
  Fruit
  Vegetables
  Beancurd
  Sauces

- Cooked Meats

- Buying Kitchen
  Utensils

Ordering Dim Sum

Dim Sum is a Cantonese style of cooking, and refers to a meal which is similar in concept to Spanish Tapas - small dishes of various descriptions. Although it is commonly believed that Dim Sum are steamed dishes, this is by no means always the case, with deep fried dishes, casseroles and stir fried dishes also available.

The Chinese often refer to Dim Sum as "Yam Char", literally "tea drinking", and indeed, the delicious dishes are accompanied by endless cups of Chinese tea. When the tea pot is empty, simply take off the teapot lid, and balance it between the rim of the teapot and teapot handle – this is the signal to the waiting staff that a refill is needed.

Whereas Yam Char has a sensible translation, Dim Sum does not. Literally it means "Dotted Heart" - meaningless. Its literal meaning is not important – Dim Sum means, well, it means Dim Sum!

The Chinese, either through necessity or through adventure, have developed a cuisine which holds almost nothing as inedible. No more is this so than in Cantonese cooking – of which Dim Sum is the finest example. But don't let what you are eating put you off – they all taste great– so try at least one adventurous dish –surprise yourself!

Vegetarian dishes are few and far between, though they do exist, and some are listed (indicated by 'V'). A great selection of fresh vegetables are always available in Chinese restaurants, though they are not generally listed on Dim Sum menus. Ask the waiter what vegetables they have, or to recommend a vegetable dish.

Family Favourites

Shrimp dumplings (har gau) A steamed half-moon shape prawn dumpling.

Pork dumplings (siu mai) Small, round steamed dumplings with a succulent pork and prawn filling.

Steamed barbecue pork buns (char siu bau)
Soft, fluffy white buns filled with Chinese barbecue pork (char siu). Steamed buns are made with a variety of other fillings, including chicken (gai) , lotus paste (lin yung) **V**, custard (lai wong) **V**, and chestnut paste (lut yung)**V**.

Curried beef crescents (gah li au so)
A curried beef filling wrapped in a flaky pastry case.

Chive dumplings (gau choi gau) Flat and round, with a chewy dough thin enough to reveal a delicate green colour on top and seared to a crisp on the other side. **V**

Spring rolls (chun geun)
Golden fried rolls filled with pork, prawns, bamboo shoots, and water chestnuts. **V**: vegetarian options are usually available.

Steamed spare ribs (pai gwat). Small tasty spare ribs steamed with black beans.

Turnip cakes (lo bak go)
Fried turnip paste with shrimp. **V**

Steamed rice rolls (cheung fan) A pasta-like dough in which prawns (ha), beef (ngau yuk) or barbecue pork (char siu) is encased. Steamed and served with a light soy sauce. For your choice, simply put the meat name in front of the dish name - for example "ha cheung fan" for the prawn variety.

Stuffed Crab Claws (yeung hai keem)
The crab meat is exposed from the claw, leaving a small part of the claw to be used as a handle. A prawn and crab paste is pressed around the claw meat, dipped in flour and bread crumbs, then deep fried.

Lotus leaf rice packets (law mai gai)
During steaming, the leaves of the lotus plant infuse their delicate flavour and aroma into a filling of glutinous rice studded with a variety of ingredients including chicken, roast pork, Chinese sausage, peanuts, and black mushrooms.

Prawn balls (ha yeung)
Prawn "meatballs".

Taro puffs (woo kok).
Deep fried
taro balls.

For The Adventurous
The following dishes are firm favourites with the Chinese - though to most non-Chinese the ingredients are enough to put them off. That's a shame, as they are in fact quite delicious.

Chicken Feet (fung jow)
Yes, these are the feet of chickens, though rather poetically called "Phoenix feet" in Chinese. These come in two popular varieties - the first is stewed in a rich sauce, and is served hot. Eating is a little cumbersome. as there are a lot of small bones. The second is a marinated version, with all the bones removed. These are more crunchy, and sometimes called Rainbow or Thai style).

Steamed Tripe (see chiu ngau pak)
A slightly spicy dish of steamed tripe in black bean and chilli sauce

Ducks Tongues (nap sit)
Marinated and steamed.

Ducks Web (nap jeyrng)
Similar to chicken's feet, but uses the feet of ducks.

Desserts
Sesame seed balls (jian dui)
Made of rice dough, these balls are filled with red bean paste and coated in sesame seeds, then deep fried. **V**

Custard tarts (don tak)
A light filo-type pastry with an egg custard-type filling. **V**

Menu Converter

The Menu Converter explains terms which you may find on a Chinese menu.

Aromatic duck

Duck served with light pancakes, cucumber, spring onions and hoi sin sauce. The duck goes through a number of cooking processes, and takes around 5 hours to cook. (Also known as Crispy Aromatic Duck)

Bean curd

Bean curd is the solid substance which is formed through the action of acid on liquidised beans. Almost tasteless in its natural state, it is highly nutritious, and often used as a meat substitute.

Black bean sauce

Sauce made from black beans and garlic. Slightly bitter, it is generally made with chillies, and so can be somewhat spicy.

Char siu

Roast pork from the south of China.

Chop suey

An Americanism for anything cooked with beansprouts as the main ingredient.

Chow mein

Literally 'fried noodles'. Cooked noodles are fried with meat and/or vegetables. "Wet" means in a sauce. "Dry" has a sauce, but minimal.

Dao fu

Cantonese for bean curd.

Dim sum

A Cantonese subset of cuisine. Dim sum is a range of small snacks, almost always steamed, and served with tea. It is a lunchtime cuisine, and eaten slowly over long conversations.

Dumplings

What the Chinese refer to as dumplings are either ravioli-type boiled 'dumplings' or else steamed buns made of a sweet dough and filled in the centre with meats or sweet fillings.

Fu Yung

An egg dish which is a cross between scrambled egg and an omelette.

Hoi sin sauce

A rich, thick, barbecue sauce

Kung Pao

A spicy hot dish made with chillies and spring onions.

Chow Mein – literally "fried noodles".

Char Siu Bao – a dim sum dish of roast pork steamed in a bun.

Ma po bean curd / Ma po dao fu
A spicy bean curd dish with minced beef in a rich thick sauce.

Mongolian hot pot
A firm favourite in northern China, the Mongolian hot pot is akin to a fondue. A 'pan' of water is heated at the table (in China this is done with a portable coal stove) and raw sliced meats and vegetables are served. The diners then cook the food themselves. The opposite of fast food, it is as much a social occasion as a meal. Sometimes called a "Steamboat".

Noodles
The original spaghetti.

Pancake roll
See spring roll.

Satay
A Malaysian dish where meat is placed on wooden skewers and deep fried. Usually served with a sauce for dipping.

Seaweed
As it suggests, seaweed. However, often some other vegetable is substituted. As it is deep fried, dry and usually salty, most people cannot tell the difference!

Sesame toast
Bread covered in a prawn based paste which is used as the adhesive to coat the bread in sesame seeds. This is then deep fried.

Shark's fin soup
Soup made from the flesh of shark's fin. A delicacy among the Chinese

Singapore fried noodles
Thin noodles with a mixture of meats and seafoods, quite spicy.

Siu mai
Steamed 'meat ball'. A dim sum dish.

Spring roll
Translated from the Chinese name, spring rolls are sheets of rice paper or a pasta type skin, filled with meat and/or vegetables and deep fried.

Sichuan style
Sichuan cooking is hot and spicy, and generally anything which is described as such will be spiked with chillies.

Won ton
A pork/prawn dumpling which is usually boiled, but can be deep fried, in which case the casing becomes crispy.

Ma Po Dao Fu– A spicy Sichuan dish.

Mongolian Hot Pot – for those with time on their hands.

At the Supermarket

Chinese fruits
Fresh Chinese or Far Eastern fruits are widely available in Chinatowns - but at a cost. These are flown in each day from the Far East. If they are in season, try some fresh lychees - well worth it.

Sharon fruit
Soft and succulent with a light fragrant taste

Long an
Literally "Dragon's Eye", a close relative to the lychee, this variety has a smooth, brown skin.

Star fruit
A "show-off" shape belies the subtle perfumed taste of this crispy fruit.

Tientsin pear
This is almost a cross between a pear and an apple. Very juicy and extremely crispy.

Pomelo
About the size of a small football, this is similar to a grapefruit, with large segments - but it is not as bitter as a grapefruit, which is thought to have been created as a cross between this fruit and an orange.

Durian
Banned in many hotels in the Far East because it is extremely malodorous- this is an acquired taste.

Kiwi
Despite popular belief, the Kiwi is native to China, and is sometimes called the Chinese gooseberry.

Mangosteen
Despite its name, not related to the mango. A sweet, soft vanilla flesh, said to be the Orang Utan's favourite food.

Mango
Quite common in supermarkets now - this fruit tastes of a mix of peaches and pineapple.

Lychee
The Chinese fruit, soft and succulent with a light fragrant taste. The pinker the skins, the fresher they are.

Chinese vegetables

Fresh Chinese vegetables are grown in glasshouses here in the UK (yes, there are Chinese-run farms in Britain) or else flown in each day from the Far East. Consequently prices may seem high. Freshness is essential, and you will see the vegetables are trimmed and cleaned.

Chinese leaf
Widely available in supermarkets now, can be used in salads, but the Chinese always fry it.

Bitter melon (Fu Gua)
The clue is in the name - this is an extremely bitter vegetable, either you love it or hate it!

Bak Choi
Also now in large supermarkets, fleshy white stalks with crisp green leaves.

Root Turnip
The root turnip is used both for its root, which is sweet and excellent for salad, soup and stir-fry, as well as for the leaves, which in many varieties can be used in stir-fryies.

Mustard leaf
Another stir fry vegetable, very slightly bitter.

Mu Li
Looks like a large white carrot, it is used in soups and casseroles, and has a very slightly hot taste.

Shanghai white
Similar to Bak Choi but with green stems and larger leaves.

Shitake mushrooms
Shitake mushrooms are usually sold dried, a process which intensifies the flavours. Fresh shitake are increasingly available.

At the Supermarket

Bottle Gourd
Picked when immature and cooked like marrows. The matured and dried fruit forms a hard wooden shell that can be used to make a drinking "bottle".

Young ginger
This is ginger that has not matured yet, and often pickled. The flavor is not as strong or as hot as common ginger.

Bamboo Shoots
Bamboo shoots are most commonly found tinned, though fresh varieties are appearing.

Winter Melon
A large melon with white flesh, a firm favourite in soups which have a disticntive flavour.

Waterchestnuts
Firm and crunchy, add crispiness to stir-fries.

Lotus root
A firm favourite in soups - adds both taste and texture.

Beancurd
Beancurd is rich is protein, vitamin B and calcium - an important source of the mineral as Chinese do not generally eat dairy products.

Soft beancurd A soft beancurd with high water content, used for soups and some stir fry dishes.

Pressed beancurd A low water content makes this beancurd far more "durable" and therefore suitable for stir frying, casseroles and stuffing.

Dried Beancurd Dried beancurd comes in many different forms, as sheets, skins, sticks or blocks. The flavour is intensified, and dried beancurd also allows texture to be introduced to a dish.

Deep Fried Beancurd
Deep fried pressed beancurd used in frying, stuffing, baking and in casseroles.

Wrapped beancurd
This beancurd is firm and contains less water than softer beancurd. Used in stir fried, steamed and stuffed dishes.

Five Spice beancurd
A flavoured beancurd which is used in stir fries as well as a dressing for cold dishes.

Beancurd puffs Soft beancurd which has been lightly deep fried. Used in stir fry dishes as well as stuffed dishes.

Sauces

There are a surprising number of sauces available on the shelves of Chinese supermarkets - from the familiar soy sauce, to the less familiar yellow bean sauce.

Chilli Sauce
A blend of chillies and fermented black beans. Spicy hot with a rich bean flavour.

Chilli Bean Sauce
Used extensively in Sichuan-style cooking, stir fries, or as a dip.

Hoi Sin Sauce
Hoi sin sauce is made from sweet potatoes, soy beans and sesame seeds. With a sweet taste this sauce is excellent for dipping, in baking and stir frying.

Light Soy Sauce
Light soy sauce is made from soybeans and brewed in China according to traditional methods. It has a full rich flavour, and is of medium saltiness.

Dark Soy Sauce
Dark soy is less salty than light soy, and in addition to being used as a condiment, is also used to colour dishes.

Oyster Sauce
Oyster sauce is used as a dip, condiment, as a gravy base or in stir frying. Oyster sauce intensifies the flavours of beef, chicken, seafood and vegetables.

Black Bean Sauce
Made from fermented black beans in a soy sauce base, ideal as a marinade, seasoning, pour-on-sauce, for stewing or steaming.

Cooked Meats

Perhaps one of the most intriguing sights in the streets of Chinatown are the numerous restaurants displaying cooked meats in their window. These meats can be "eaten in", or may be bought to take home. Although home cooking is the norm, these meats are, in general, prepared in very time intensive ways, and therefore are a popular alternative to cooking at home for those who find their life too busy. For a quick snack, jut add some boiled rice, and– an instant meal!

Perhaps the most disconcerting aspect of these items is the Chinese custom of very often leaving the entire animal intact while cooking - therefore head and feet are often in place, and as can be seen from the picture above, a whole squid is cooked, despite its size!

When buying cooked meats, the restaurant will gladly cut or slice it, just ask. Equally, you can also ask for a portion of sauce - made from a light soy sauce base, this is an excellent accompaniment to add a delicious flavour to rice.

1. Belly pork with crackling
Belly pork which has been roasted, and has crunchy crackling on top.

2. Steamed chicken
Steaming the chicken ensures that all the moisture is retained, giving succulent meat.

3. Soy chicken
These chickens are marinated in a light soy sauce marinade before being steamed, giving a full flavoured, succulent taste.

4. Barbecue roast pork
A firm favourite, the pork is barbecued. Commonly called by its Cantonese name - Char Siu.

5. Squid
A little chewy, but always delicious.

6. Roast duck
Again, along with char siu, a firm favourite. The skin is crispy but very light.

Equipment and Utensils

Wok (A)

Not surprisingly, the most important piece of equipment in the Chinese kitchen is the wok, a thin metal frying pan. The wok has deep sides and a curved bottom designed to spread the heat evenly around the whole surface.

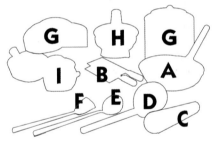

Woks come with either one long handle or two wooden (occasionally metal) side-handles, the first type for stir-frying, the second for steaming or deep-frying. Woks are fairly inexpensive – the long-handled sort is best for general use, and are best bought from a Chinese supermarket or other Chinatown shop if possible. Fancy woks with elaborate plastic fittings, or 'non-stick' ones, sold in department stores as 'wok sets' are generally inferior in every way.

Once you have your wok, it needs to be seasoned before use. To season a wok, rinse it in water, dry it, then heat it slowly for ten minutes or so wiped with a little oil (use some kitchen roll to do this); let it cool, and wipe the wok, repeating the whole process until clean kitchen paper wipes clean. After some use, the interior surface of the wok will turn black. This is fine: never clean it with detergent; always use plain water and dry thoroughly before rubbing it with a little oil. If it rusts, scrub it off and season the wok again before use.

Wok lid and stand

Many elaborate lists of 'essential' equipment for Chinese cooking are available; however alongside your wok, the only other equipment you need for basic Chinese cooking is a large lid for the wok (for use when steaming) and a wok stand, which makes a base for the wok over the gas flame or electric ring.

Wok Brush (C)

These are used to clean the wok simply with some elbow grease and a little water.

Spatulas, ladels etc (D, E, F)

Spatulas and other common kitchen utensils can be used comfortably with Chinese cooking. If you intend to cook Chinese food often, a long-handled metal spatula, a sieve, ladel and wooden chopsticks will prove useful.

Steamers (G)

Steamers, which are placed on a little metal stand inside a water-filled wok . Traditionally made of bamboo, they may also be found made of metal.

Chopping knives(B)

Because knives are not used at Chinese dining tables, food is cut during cooking preparation. Both meat cleavers as well as fruit and vegetable knives are available.

Steamboat (H)

Traditional 'fondue' style steamer, sometimes known as the Mongolian hot pot which is used at the table. Traditionally fuelled with charcoal, but electric versions are available.

Soup/Casserole Pots (I)

Used for boiling, simmering and stewing.

倫敦

萬國之城

London
City of Ten Thousand Nations

Liverpool boasts Europe's oldest Chinatown but, it was in fact to London that the first Chinese came to in Britain. The arrival of Shen Fu-Tsung in the 1681 (see page 8), Chinese sailors were in London from the last quarter of the 1700s. *Gentleman's Magazine* reported a disturbance among 500 Chinese sailors in the East India Company's barracks at King David's Fort in Shadwell East London in October 1813, but we know that Chinese sailors were here much earlier from the life of John Anthony (see page 8)

Britain's victory over China in the Opium Wars increased trade between the two countries. Nonetheless, by 1941, some 100 years later, there were still only about 30 Chinese businesses in the Limehouse area of London. These Chinese had begun settling in the area from the 1850s onwards. Despite their relatively small numbers, their impact was suffi-cient for the area to become known as Chinatown. These busi-nesses served the tran-sient population of Chinese sailors.

London's modern-day Chinatown is no longer in Limehouse, and almost 100 years further on London now boasts over 3,000 Chinese business-es and a Chinese population of around 100,000.

The development of the area we now know as Chinatown can be traced back to the Great Fire of London in 1666 In just a few short days 13,000 homes were destroyed
a n d

well over 100,000 of London's more affluent residents were made homeless. Attention turned to the area around present day Soho because of its proximity to the three palaces of Westminster, Whitehall and St James. Soho was on the up!

Nicholas Barbon acquired a building lease from Lord Gerrard in 1677 Barbon completed the construction of Gerrard Street in 1685, by which time he had also acquired the near-by estate belonging to Lord Newport. Here he developed more houses and a large market.

Sadly the area never retained its initial grandeur, and had become run down by the mid 18th century. It became home for successive waves of immigrant communities, French (the Huguenot church on nearby Orange Street is the oldest in the country), Italian and Jewish.

Limehouse was severely damaged by bombing during the 1940s and the Chinese found themselves, like many in those days, displaced. The Chinese dispersed, but were destined to regroup once the new home of Soho emerged.

Gerrard Street in the late 50s was a shabby street. As a result, property prices were very cheap, and short leases could be found for next to nothing. At the same time thousands of agricultural workers from Hong Kong, forced out of their traditional occupations by changes in the world rice markets, began to arrive in Britain. With the booming catering trade, these new immigrants found immediate employment, often with tied accommodation as restaurants and takeaways sprang up in every major city and town in the country.

Getting There

Situated in Soho in the heart of central London, London Chinatown is within easy walking distance of Tottenham Court Road, Oxford Street, Charing Cross Road, Trafalgar Square and Piccadilly Circus. It is well served by public transport links, and is easiest reached by tube.

Driving to London Chinatown is not recommended. Car parking is available, although both car parks are frequently full in the daytime, and charge hefty Central London prices.

Tube & Rail

Less than a minute's walk from Chinatown is Leicester Square (Northern & Piccadilly lines) tube station. Also within walking distance:

• Piccadilly Circus
(Piccadilly & Bakerloo lines)
• Oxford Circus
(Victoria, Central & Bakerloo lines)
• Tottenham Court Road
(Central & Northern lines)
• Charing Cross
(Bakerloo, Jubilee & Northern lines)

The nearest overground main line station is Charing Cross.

Bus

Buses that take you to within easy walking distance of Chinatown are: 3, 6, 7, 8, 9, 10, 11, 12, 13, 14, 15, 19, 22, 23, 24, 25, 29, 38, 53, 55, 73, 77a, 88, 89, 91, 94, 134, 139, 159, 176, 242.

**London Transport Information
020 7222 1234**

With the influx of Chinese, and the substantial business success of the catering trade, associated businesses, designed to cater for restaurant workers, grew up on Gerrard Street, which became known as Chinatown. More families were reunited as wives and children joined their husbands.

The relative educational success of British Born Chinese brought further economic success, and the Chinese by and large moved out of Chinatown, making room for more commercial space, and went to the suburbs.

Chinatown itself was transformed by Westminster City Council, recognising that it had become a major tourist attraction. Gerrard Street was pedestrianised in the 1980s, as was part of Newport Place and Macclesfield Street. Chinese-style gateways, street furniture and a pavilion were added as Chinatown came of age, a symbol of the success as well as a cultural focal point of the Chinese community of London.

Despite its short history, London's Chinatown has, perhaps, seen the most significant changes of any Chinatown in Britain. Driven by economic imperatives, the business landscape has over the past decade or so, narrowed significantly. Astronomical rents have seen many of the quirkier businesses which can

In 2002 the Chinese New Year celebrations in London were Europe's largest, and were the first officially sanctioned "private" celebrations ever to take place in Trafalgar Square.

be found in Britain's other Chinatown's driven out. For its size, there are relatively few arts and crafts stores, for example. Many such businesses were lost, having been replaced by the ever increasing number of restaurants – one of the few businesses which have sufficiently high turnovers to pay the rent and business rates demanded in prime central London commercial property. Anyone in any doubt over the higher costs involved need only park their car in either of the two car parks in Chinatown while they have lunch – expect little change from £20!

It has to be said, the lack of diversity in the retail outlets in Chinatown is something which is a little sad. One of the great attractions of shopping in Chinatown in Manchester, Liverpool, Birmingham or Newcastle is exploring the shops that stock "odd items". In London, the need to make every square foot of retail space earn its keep has driven a lot of that out – proprietors preferring to stock safe, high turnover items. But all is not lost, there are still a few gems to be found – it just takes a little bit more effort.

The Guardian Lions

The two lions which face out of Chinatown, and protect the approach to Gerrard Street from Macclesfield Street were donated as a gift to the people of London by the government of China.

They were unveiled by the Duke of Gloucester in 1985 as part of the ceremony that officially opened the pedestrianisation of Chinatown and the installation of the Chinese Gates. There's a plaque which details the various dignitaries who attended.

There is a second plaque on top of the main plinth on which the lions sit. This records the visit of the Prince of Wales to Chinatown in 2000.

The visit by the Prince was seen as an attempt to mend bridges between the Royal household and the Chinese community after Prince Charles' refusal to attend a state banquet for the visiting Premier of China, Jiang Zemin was widely interpreted as a deliberate snub.

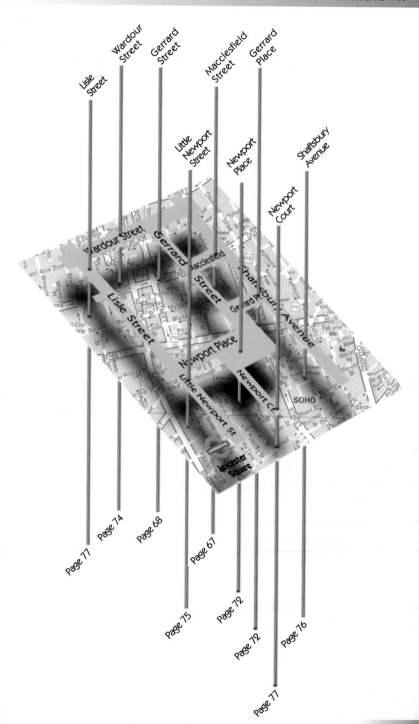

Lisle Street

Wardour Street

Gerrard Street

Macclesfield Street

Gerrard Place

Little Newport Street

Newport Place

Shaftsbury Avenue

Newport Court

London Chinatown Gateways

Perhaps the most distinctive feature of London's Chinatown are the three steel Chinese 'gateways' that mark the entrances to Gerrard Street from the east, west and north.

Standing at an imposing 8m the gates were made by London based firm Comyn Ching and are a modern representation of a traditional Chinese archway – such archways commonly being erected in China, both in days gone by, and increasingly in modern times, in commercial areas. (For an explanation of the origins and meaning of gateways, see page 93).

The gates themselves have various texts on them, though the logic of how these texts are arranged is something of a mystery. At the southern end of Gerrard Street the text only appears on one side, while at the northern end the texts are not only on both sides, but differ on each side.

The principle text at the top of each gate as one enters Gerrard Street (shown above) reads "lun dun wah fao", (Cantonese) which literally translates as London Chinese District or more loosely London Chinatown.

One point which is worth noting is the direction in which the Chinese text is written. In classical Chinese, characters are written in a vertical direction, from top to bottom, and from

London Chinatown Gatesways

the right hand side of the page to the left. For this reason many people believe the Chinese read from right to left. However, when written horizontally, the text reads from left to right, just as in English.

Although the text at the top of the gate is horizontal, and therefore would normally read from left to right, in this instance, it reads the opposite way. The reason for this is that the two vertical statements on each side of the gate set the direction of reading the Chinese on the gate.

It is common practice for the first characters of these plaques to have a message in themselves. Therefore, as can be seen from the images of the plaques, the four sentences start with the four characters "lun dun hua fao"- the same phrase as written on the main horizontal plaque.

The texts are difficult to give exact translations to as they are poetic. The following are very much paraphrases.

The general meaning of the first pair of texts (shown alongside) is:

The second pair roughly translates as:

"The Chinese will uphold honesty and good public order"

and

'Wishing health and prosperity in Westminster City".

The reverse text on the top of the gates (shown below) reads "feng tiao yu sun" a paraphrase is:

"May the wind blow favourably, and rain fall at the right time"

It is a wish for wealth and prosperity.

"We came from afar to the garden of the great British nation"

and

"Wishing that the Chinese community's friendship with others grows from strength to strength."

What's it all about?
The Chinese language, although not unique, is one of a very small group of languages in which the written form does not vary with different spoken forms. Therefore, although a Cantonese speaker listening to a Mandarin speaker may not understand anything that is said, he or she could *read* the most complex and technical of speeches and understand everything.

If the written form of the language is complex, the spoken variations are just as staggering. There are eight major language groups with some 600 dialects - all sharing the same written form. There are a further 136 non-Chinese languages spoken in China. All Chinese languages use tones to distinguish different words.

London Chinatown's Pavilion

In Newport Place sits the perfectly proportioned Chinese pavilion, sitting on top of its hexagonal base. The Chinese pavilion was manufactured in China, and assembled by a team of craftsmen from China back in 1983

The pavilion sits on a six-sided base, with the roof resting on six red pillars. It is interesting that the pavilion is of a hexagonal shape, and this indicates that this is in fact a small structure - the preferred shape is octagonal because of the positive associations of the number eight (see page 113). A larger structure would have been out of character in such a small space, and undoubtedly this is why this 'small' size was chosen.

The roof tiles are in traditional (Ming) yellow, and each of the six corners curves in the typical Chinese fashion. This curve is not only aesthetic, but serves as a defence against evil. It was believed that demons could only fly in straight lines (the reason why traditional Chinese homes require a right angle turn to enter). As the roof eves were a potential entry point, they were curved, and for good measure, guardian creatures were used to protect this entry point. In this case, even though it is clearly an open structure, the traditional design principles are maintained.

There are five griffins which protect the pavilion. The number of guardian creatures of a

The traditional colours of good luck and fortune - red and gold - make up the colour scheme. Between the pillars classical Chinese fretwork designs can be seen. Traditionally these would be made of wood, though the base material for this modern construction is concrete. Above the fretwork are traditional Chinese designs which were hand painted onto the base once the pavilion was erected.

structure is always odd, as odd numbers are 'yang' (masculine) and therefore more potent in warding off evil. The higher the status of the building, the more guardian creatures, up to nine, which was reserved for the Emperor's buildings.

Love them or hate them, the pavilion's classical roof line is bedecked with multicoloured lightbulbs which are lit in the hours of darkness.

Macclesfield Street is the modern name of an old road built to provide access to the mansion of Charles Gerrard, Earl of Macclesfield. The mansion has long since gone, but the road's use as an entry point has not. The southern gates to Chinatown sit on Macclesfield Street, and this is the grandest way to enter.

As a short street, there are just a handful of Chinese businesses here. That said , they include one of Chinatown's two Chinese bookshops (Chung Ying), a travel agency (above the bookshop) as well as a bakery and four restaurants.

Dansey Place runs off Macclesfield Street. Dansey place is little more than the service alley for premises which front Gerrard Street and Shaftsbury Avenue. It is home to Chinatown's oldest Chinese printers, Pang's Printing, and in recent years some meat and vegetable wholesalers have set up shop here, servicing the restaurant trade.

This is the only place in Chinatown where you can really get an idea of the complex air extraction systems used in restaurant kitchens. Although the number of restaurants on Gerrard Street backing onto Dansey Place is relatively low, the ductwork is very prominent.

Memory Lane

The Horse and Dolphin Yard, taking its name from the tavern that stood there for more than 300 years, lies just off Macclesfield Street. The tavern was demolished in 1890 as part of the road widening scheme which created Shaftsbury Avenue and was rebuilt, but was named the Macclesfield Arms, and subsequently became De Hems (London's only "Dutch Pub").

The strange name combination of Horse and Dolphin refers to the posts used for tethering a horse to: these were called dolphins, hence horse and dolphin.

Many visitors to Chinatown get a smell of the place before they actually get sight of it. These ducts (of which there are literally dozens in a very small area) are the source of the aroma - though their purpose is to actually take the smells away, high above street level - imagine how strong the aromas would be if they weren't present!

What's it all about?

A pavilion (ting) is a garden structure. They are clearly aesthetically pleasing to look at, though they are in fact intended more to be looked out of, rather than into.

Chinese gardens were designed with specific purposes in mind, and one key purpose was as a place of contemplation. Pavilions were places for such contemplation, often built at strategically panoramic points. Equally they could be used for a whole range of activities from calligraphy to playing chess.

Lakeside pavilion, Shanghai, China

Gerrard Street is the heart of London Chinatown, with everything from a Chinese bank through to hairstylists, craft shops and music stores, and home to some of Europe's finest Chinese restaurants.

It is ironic that the success of Chinatown is also one of its greatest threats, and year on year more and more retailing space is lost to restaurants as they steadily take over of the area. The truth is that very few businesses can compete with restaurants when it comes to returns on investment, and in a community where enterprise is king (The Chinese are three times more likely than their British white counterparts to be self employed), it is profitability which matters. Sadly that has meant the loss of some of the more 'colourful' shops, though it is still possible to find the unusual among all the restaurants.

Gerrard Street truly is the heart of the Chinese community. It is the only street in the UK (and probably Europe) in which you could pick up a paper in Chinese, read the news over coffee and a pastry, have your haircut, eat a world class dim sum lunch, have an afternoon flutter on the horses, book a holiday, find a new home, talk over the details with a solicitor, invest on the stock exchange, pick up the latest CD, talk to your accountant, print your wedding stationery, buy a bonsai tree, consult a Chinese herbalist, browse through a bookshop, open a bank account and enjoy the activities of the local community centre **and** do all this only using the Chinese language.

Nowhere in Europe is there a street with a greater choice of Chinese cuisine, and nowhere to match the sheer quality of the food prepared.

Gerrard Street is not only a symbol of the success of the Chinese in Britain, but is also a street of which Britain can be proud: a truly inspirational achievement of multi-cultural Britain, for not only does the street serve as a service and retailing centre for the Chinese, but it also acts as an enormous open air classroom for the tens of thousands of visitors who walk down it each day.

Unlike the Uk's other Chinatowns, Gerrard Street remains almost free of Chinese style canopies, at least on shop fronts. Much of this is due to the fact that London's Chinatown lies in the middle of a conservation area, and the local authority enforce strict conditions on the facias which are allowed. Despite heavy restrictions on the frontages of the shops, there is an abundance of street furniture, from bollards to traffic control gates. These are all of a modern design, and in traditional Chinese colours of green and red. Surprisingly the effort to keep the original shop fronts (or what remains of them) together with a very modern interpretation of ancient Chinese themes actually works quite well, providing an ambience which is neither overbearing nor oversterile. One exception, has to be (and this won't be the only time this is mentioned) the public telephone boxes. Ten out of ten for effort, a big fat zero for results. The plastic "pagoda" telephone boxes are too tacky for words, and the "Hong Kong Phooey" style writing almost an insult. It's something which needs to be done properly, or not done at all, and many believe these eyesores need to go.

It has to be said, Gerrard Street is a little bit touristy, but that's not necessarily a bad thing - it brings custom to the Chinese businesses, provides tourists with some of the best Chinese cuisine outside of Asia, and, by and large, encourages an interest in Chinese culture and heritage. Its as close as you'll get to the Far East for about 8,000 miles!

Gerrard Street has had many famous residents as well as, in days gone by, being the home of one of Britain's most well known household names.

Gerrard Street was built between 1677 and 1685 and is named after the Earls of Macclesfield, the Gerrards whose mansion was previously close by.

Gerrard Street was initially distinguished by its aristocratic inhabitants. From the mid eighteenth century it was better known for its taverns and coffee houses. In the first half of the twentieth century it became well known for its night clubs and in the 1950s for its striptease clubs.

Number 9 Gerrard Street, was the home of The Literary Club at what was the Turks Head Tavern. The Literary Club was founded by Joshua Reynolds and Samuel Johnson in 1764 and was probably the most famous of the literary and theatrical clubs in London.

Number 22 is where James Boswell (1740-95) the biographer of the lexicographer Samuel Johnson lodged with a tailor in 1775

Number 37was the home of Edmund Burke between 1787-90. He wrote his famous critique of the French Revolution *Reflections on the Revolution in France* here.

Memory Lane

Number 39 was one of the first working men's clubs. The basement of this building was the original setting for Ronnie Scott's jazz club which opened in 1959, and later moved to Frith Street.

Number 43 is the site of a house in which John Dryden, essayist and author of the neoclassical criticism of Shakespeare, An *Essay of Dramatic Poesy* (1668), lived between 1687 and 1700

Andrew Pears opened premises in Gerrard Street in 1789 where he manufactured and sold various soaps and powders to the wealthy inhabitants of the area, and so began the world famous, iconic Pear's Soap.

Newport Place

It's interesting to note that West Central has opted to include a Chinese version of its name above its door, with the added explanation in smaller characters that it is a gay pub. Gay has been translated using colloquial Cantonese, which in formal Chinese actually translates as "Comrade" - perhaps this is an oversight, but its quite an amusing one! It does emphasise how the Chinese live in harmony with the fantastic diversity that is London. There are now no fewer than five pubs in Chinatown.

Newport Place was once the venue for the Chinese New Year celebrations stage, but the days when it was anywhere near big enough have long since gone, and the stage is now in Leicester Square, and in 2002 an even larger stage was erected in Trafalgar Square with a live television link between the two.

There is also an underground car park which is entered via Newport Place. It is extremely convenient for Chinatown, but beware, parking rates are high, even by London standards. There is a reduced flat rate for evening visitors entering after a certain time (check the latest position with NCP), and this can save anything up to an hour of frustration searching for a car park space in the early evening.

If Chinatown is a small village in a big city, then Newport Place has to be the village green. Newport Place offers Chinatown at least something of a semblance of a public space, and the pavilion in its centre is perfectly proportioned (see page 66).

Despite having a seven metre high solid brick wall along the entire length of its north side, Newport Place manages to pack in a great variety of businesses including a music shop, bookshop, fishmongers, two supermarkets, a tea shop, two travel agents, an estate agent, a bookmakers, two Japanese restaurants, a Chinese restaurant and two pubs, including Chinatown's very own gay pub, West Central.

> **Gerrard Place**
> Gerrard Place lies at the eastern end of Gerrard Street, and links Gerrard Street and Newport Place with Shaftsbury Avenue. This is home to just one restaurant, the New World, which has stood there for many, many years. Beyond that, there are a number of the plastic pagoda-style roof telephone boxes almost universally disliked. Being so close to the last bastion of London's central red light district, these telephone boxes are often festooned with the "calling cards" of escorts of every description, and as such, best avoided, particularly if you're visiting Chinatown with younger children.

Wardour Street

Wardour Street is at the western end of Gerrard Street and links Shaftsbury Avenue with (ultimately) Trafalgar Square. It is perhaps better known as a centre of the British film distribution industry (this is centred to the north of Shaftsbury Avenue), and will have many a fond memory for those who enjoyed their youth in 60s 'Swinging London'.

South of Shaftsbury Avenue, Wardour Street is well and truly incorporated into Chinatown. Here again we see how Chinatown exists happily with its neighbours from different communities: London's Dutch pub (De Hems on Macclesfield Street), West Central (gay pub) in Newport Place and here in Wardour Street, the Swiss Centre.

Wardour Street is one of the traditional boundary streets of Chinatown, although these days Chinese businesses have moved further afield, and there are also some businesses to be found off Wardour Street in Rupert Place.

The businesses themselves on Wardour Street include an electronics company (handy for electric rice cookers), a Chinese pharmacy and a number of restaurants. One restaurant to note is the Chuen Cheng Ku with its magnificent Dragon totem above the entrance.

Chinese Dragon Totem outside the Chuen Cheng Ku Restaurant

Little Newport Street

What's it all about?

The Chinese dragon, unlike its western cousin, is considered to be a benevolent creature, the custodian of rain, rivers and lakes, and a harbinger of good fortune.

In Chinese mythology the dragon is described as having the body of a snake, the face of a horse, antlers of the deer and claws of the eagle. The dragon also has the beard of a goat and the scales of a fish.

One explanation of how the dragon came to be suggests early societies had as their tribal mascot an animal - for example a horse or a camel or a fish (this is in fact something which we observe even today with the American eagle, the British lion or the Russian bear). These symbols were used both for religious as well as military purposes, and rather as the Romans would march with the eagle on their standards, these emblems were used as military insignia. As a tribe went to battle and conquered another, it would incorporate some form of the conquered tribe's insignia. In this way it is believed the Xia clan, who had a snake as its emblem annexed states such as the Shang - an eagle. Thus, to the snake's body was added the claws of the eagle. Soon the scales of fish, antlers of the deer, face of the horse and the beard of the goat all came to be incorporated, and thereby the Chinese dragon came into being.

So powerful did the emblem of the dragon become that it was adopted by every Chinese dynasty as the Imperial emblem.

Newport Court and Little Newport Street run parallel to each other off Newport Place. Little Newport Street is the road you are most likely to walk up if you arrive at Leicester Square underground station. It has businesses on one side of the street, the other being flanked by the northern facade of the Hippodrome complex. This is the only street in Chinatown which

Little Newport Street

does not have a Chinese restaurant (there is in fact a restaurant, but it is Japanese).

The lack of restaurants is more than made up for by the diversity of other businesses, including a tea shop, travel agents, two herbalists, a newspaper agency, Chinatown's only martial arts shop and one of Britain's oldest Chinese societies, the Kung Ho Association which shares the street with one of Britain's newer Chinese associations, The Chinese Sports Association.

Shaftsbury Avenue

Shaftsbury Avenue is a relative new-comer to the claims of Chinatown. Although there have been Chinese businesses here for some time, they were few. Ten years ago the Mayflower Restaurant, the Bank of East Asia and the Bank of China were the only Chinese businesses visible. There have, however, been service industries such as accountants, solicitors and so on in the offices above the shops for just as long. More recently a number of Chinese business have spread into Shaftsbury Avenue as space within the traditional area of Chinatown is limited, and rents extraordinarily high.

The arrival of the Dao Heng Bank really makes this the 'financial' centre of Chinatown, although the Hong Kong Bank (part of the HSBC group - it is not widely known that the initials HSBC originally stood for Hong Kong and Shanghai Banking Corporation) retains offices in Gerrard Street.

The acknowledgement that Shaftsbury Avenue had become part of Chinatown proper came in 2000 when the procession routes for the Chinese Lion dances during Chinese New Year included Shaftsbury Avenue.

Shaftsbury Avenue is named after the Seventh Earl of Shaftsbury (1801-1885). Lord Shaftsbury was one of Britain's greatest social reformers. He worked strenuously to alleviate poverty, and brought about the Factory Acts (1847, 1850 and 1859), and the Coal Mines Act (1842) which stopped the employment of women and children under 13 underground .

Shaftsbury was a friend of the famous slavery abolitionist William Wilberforce and also Florence Nightingale, helping with her army welfare and nursing work, and was centrally involved in the YMCA and YWCA.

Memory Lane

The Avenue was opened in 1886, taking the route of existing streets, though many had to be widened, and it is perhaps fitting that in the process of building Shaftsbury Avenue it was necessary to demolish a large number of slums of which Shaftsbury worked so tirelessly to eliminate.

Lisle Street is London Chinatown's second major street, though once again, it only really has businesses on one side. This time the southern side of the street is almost entirely taken up by the imposing solid brick back wall of the Odeon multiplex cinema on Leicester Square.

Lisle Street is mainly occupied by restaurants, although there is also a Chinese herbalist and two supermarkets. The narrowness of the pavement on Lisle Street makes walking down this street a slow process, not assisted by being hemmed in by parked cars.

Many of the restaurants on this street are smaller and more intimate than those found in Gerrard Street.

The Skin Hospital was situated on Lisle Street, and its impressive facade can still be seen. The hospital closed as recently as the late 1990s and is now occupied by a "trendy wine bar" (it's not just banks then. But then there must surely be some connection between skincare and skinfulls).

Newport Court

Newport Court is an alleyway which links Charing Cross Road with Newport Place.

Here, there's a mix of Chinese and non-Chinese businesses like nowhere else in Chinatown, though the Chinese businesses are slowly becoming more dominant. There's a catering supply store here (Newport Kitchen Supplies) which carries woks, steamers and the like as well as a good range of Japanese and Chinese tableware.

Manchester
City of Aspirations

曼徹斯特

夢想之城

It was in the 1500s that the weaving of cloth became important to Manchester. The connection with the wool trade developed to include cotton which became the mainstay of Manchester's industry in the 18th, 19th and 20th centuries. It was during the 19th century that Manchester became a world leader in industrial output, and second only to London in terms of commercial importance.

Manchester's Chinatown lies in the very heart of the city in the area that known as Picadilly. As Manchester developed the area was not a fashionable part of town. However, the rise of the area was brought about as a consequence of the Glorious Revolution (1688) in which the Roman Catholic King James II was deposed, and replaced by his daughter, the protestant Mary and her husband, William of Orange.

Supporters of James were known as pro-Jacobites (from the Latin for James: Jacob). When Queen Anne came to the throne in 1702 the pro-Jacobite movement was still strong, and Anne made a concerted effort to consolidate her Protestant rule in Manchester by erecting a new church to rival the strongly Jacobite Collegiate church of St James in St James Square. St Anne's church was built in St Anne's Square which lies to the Northwest of Chinatown. The area quickly became the height of fashion with significant development over the next hundred years. It was in 1788 that both George Street and Charlotte Street developed as very fashionable streets – as indicated by their Royal names (Queen Charlotte and King George).

As with many of Britain's great cities, it all started with the Romans. The Roman fort of "Mamucium" was established in 70AD as part of the occupation of Britain. The fort was strategically placed on the junction of the Irwell and the Medlock rivers, and on the road between Chester and York.

With the departure of the Romans in 410AD, Mamucium developed very little until the 10th century when the Saxons rebuilt it as a defence against marauding Vikings. They renamed it "Manceastre" and it was to develop into a market town and an important centre for the wool trade. In 1303 it was granted the Great Charter of Manchester, becoming a free borough.

The Chinese first arrived in Manchester in the early part of the 20th century. Proximity to Liverpool made Manchester the most natural place for the Chinese to expand into. The Chinese came as individuals, engaged in what had become the traditional trade of the Chinese – laundry. It wasn't until the 1940s that Chinese arrived in greater numbers, and even then, numbered under one hundred. The first Chinese restaurant to open in Manchester did so in 1948, the Ping Hong in Mosley Street. Over the next twelve years sixteen more restaurants were to open. The boom continued well into the 60s and 70s. In 1962 the Willow Garden (now closed) opened with a capacity of 600.

The area around Faulkner Street has always been a location in which the Chinese have established businesses, way back to the Ping Hong in 1948. However, applying the term Chinatown to the area became apt only in the 70s with the establishment of restaurants such as Charlie Chan's (1973), the Woo Sang (1976) and the Little Yang Sing (1978).

Chinatown "status" was officially recognised when the Duke of Edinburgh unveiled the replica Ming Dynasty Imperial Arch that straddles Nicholas and Faulkner Streets. Britain's first Chinese Arts centre opened its doors in Charlotte Street in 1989 (it has since relocated) and for a while Manchester was giving London a good run for its money. Some will still argue that Manchester holds Britain's most exciting, vibrant Chinese community.

Getting There

Situated just to the southwest of Picadilly Gardens, Manchester's Chinatown is readily reached by public transport.

Although there is a carpark in the heart of Manchester Chinatown it is relatively small and can get full very early on in the day. Other car parks are clearly signposted in the wider area. Street parking is also available.

By Rail

National Rail station Manchester Picadilly is just a 15 minute walk away. Walk out of the station and down the hill (London Road). London Road becomes Picadilly, which in turn leads to Picadilly Gardens. Follow the road around to the left (Portland Street). Nicholas Street is the fourth on the right.

By Coach

Charlotte Street Coach station is 2 minutes walk from Chinatown. Walk north-westerly along Sackville Street, then cross Portland Street into Nicholas Street.

By Bus and Metrolink

As Picadilly Gardens is the hub of Manchester bus network we have not listed the bus numbers that stop there. Similarly Picadilly Gardens is a major hub for the Manchester Metrolink system. Chinatown is less than a five minute walk from Picadilly Gardens, just to the South West.

**Manchester Visitor Information Centre
0161 236 9900**

Chinese New Year
London

Chinatown Online
Britain's premiere web site on all things Chinese

chinatown-online.co.uk

Chinatown Online - Promoting Chinese
culture online, on paper and on the ground

www.chinatown-online.co.uk

Faulkner Street

Nicholas Street

George Street

Page 89

Page 88

Page 86

Manchester had seen nothing like it – indeed, Britain had seen nothing like it. Spanning a British Street was a faithful replica of an Ming Dynasty Imperial Arch, resplendent in gold, green and red, and adorned with dragons and phoenix and various symbols of good luck and prosperity.

Completed on 17th April 1987, Manchester's Imperial Arch was Europe's first, and wasn't done in half measures! Although proudly standing at an impressive 11.5m in Manchester, the arch began life in Beijing where its constituent parts were made by the Beijing Landscape and Classical Architectural Company.

These were loaded into no fewer than three containers and shipped to Manchester where 12 skilled craftsmen from the same company laboured seven days a week for almost four months constructing and then decorating the arch, which technically is in the "Dragon Grass Seal Style".

Construction was no easy task: problems obtaining visas for the craftsmen meant that the work had to be completed during the winter instead of the summer.

Needless to say Manchester's winter months proved damp if not wet, and this caused endless problems with the paint drying - it wouldn't! A warm air fan was brought in and although it assisted the paint in drying, it also caused dust to be blown onto the paint. One panel had to be painted no fewer than six times before the craftsmen were happy with it. This probably says more about the arch than anything else - it was never enough simply to be good, it had to be perfect.

The total cost of the Arch was £350,000, £125,000 of which was a gift from the government of the People's Republic of China. The rest came from various local authority agencies including Manchester City Council, The Department of the Environment and a contribution from the local Chinese community.

After twelve year's of Manchester's weather, the Arch had a extensive refurbishment in 2002, bringing it back to its original glory.

What's it all about?

The construction of archways in China dates back hundreds of years. Imperial permission to construct an archway was necessary, and such permission was considered a great privilege. Arches appear in front of temples, tombs, villages and important centres of commerce where quite often the merchants of rival towns would seek to build the most impressive arch in their region

Archways are not merely ornamental, but were also believed to bring good fortune, and are often inscribed with words invoking success or good wishes. Symbols placed on the arches were equally significant.

A 17th century five-roof arch in Yunan, Anhui Province, China

Colours: There are three main colours on the arch. Gold is the colour of fame, progress and advancement, red the colour of good fortune and green the colour of life and peace.

Dragons: The dragon is a Chinese symbol of authority and power. It was an emblem of the Emperor, and when representing the Emperor, the dragon always had five talons. Four-taloned dragons are 'common or garden' dragons. Being an Imperial arch the decorations on the Manchester archway have five talons.

Phoenix: The phoenix is a symbol of peace and prosperity. It is seen as the "opposite" of the dragon in sense of Yin and Yang (see page 21), therefore whereas the dragon is very masculine, the phoenix is seen as feminine. Together the dragon and phoenix represent harmony, balance and peaceful co-existence.

Flowers: The first botanical gardens were established in China 100 years before the birth of Christ, and flowers have always held a special place in Chinese culture. Almost all flowers have a symbolic meaning, and quite often their representation is so stylised as to make recognition to the untrained eye quite difficult. One reason for this is that the flowers are traditionally drawn with a perspective "from above". Try to spot the Peony "fu" which sounds exactly the same as the word for good fortune. Also look out for the lotus - a symbol of purity and perfection because it grows out of mud, and yet is not soiled. As a symbol of fruitfulness, the lotus symbolises the bestowing of gifts, those gifts being the virtues represented by the other symbols - peace, harmony and prosperity.

Tile figures: seen on the eaves of the five roofs, these are mythical figures intended to ward off evil. The man sitting on a cockerel at the very front represents the Emperor. The cockerel represents courage, and being at the front, the Emperor is seen as the ultimate protector against evil.

The inscription at the top of the Arch reads from left to right Man Chi Xi Te zhong guo cheng" (Mandarin): Manchester Chinatown

and the landscaping which has been undertaken along Faulkner Street. This is easy to miss from the street as it is almost always hidden behind the street parked cars which arrive early and don't disappear until the small hours of the morning.

Home to Manchester's oldest supermarket, Wing Fat, the street is always busy with shoppers, and the adjacent Tung Sing Housing Project (for the elderly) gives visitors to Manchester Chinatown a feeling that this is actually a local community rather than just a business centre.

Being Chinatown's "Main Street", there are of course lots of restaurants, and in common with other Chinatown's these are no longer only Chinese, but include other Asian cuisines.

In addition to restaurants there are now many other shops from arts and crafts to printing, jewellery to a Chinese bakery. Many an hour can be lost as you browse the stores along Faulkner Street.

Faulkner Street is the heart of Manchester Chinatown, but as one side of half of the street is taken up by a car park, it gives the impression that Chinatown is a little disjointed - and strangely makes what is in fact a fairly compact area of just three main streets seem quite spread out.

Another quirky feature of the street is the half-basement design of many of the shops (and those in many of the surrounding streets). This is a throw-back to the days when almost all the building here were converted into warehouses.

Even if you don't have a car, its worth going into the car park, as this offers the best views of the Imperial Arch

Memory Lane

Faulkner Street has had many notable residents, and seems to have been a favourite with scientific institutions. In 1815 the Eye Institute was housed at number 35, in 1838 the first home of the Manchester Geological Society was set up at number 25, and number 40 was home to Thomas Turner, President of the first medical school to be based outside of London.

As late as 1833 a man called William Scott kept 3 pig sties in Faulkner Street - described at the time as "the residence of lodging house keepers, book keepers, ministers, artists and owners of academies."

George Street

George Street runs parallel to Faulkner Street, on the opposite side of the central carpark. It was the first street to be occupied by Chinese in today's Chinatown, and home to Chinatown's oldest surviving restaurant, Charlie Chans (opened 1973).

Landscaping continues on the car park side of the street. The landscaping was designed by the City Council's engineering department, back in 1986, which chose plants from China such as jasmine, maples, cherries, junipers and bamboos, as well as natural rock formations and secluded seating for rest and contemplation. You will have to arrive early for contemplation however, as noise levels are usually high during the day. The overall effect of the landscaping is good, though some may say that there isn't the space that would do it justice. This is probably a fair comment, but given the lack of space, the result is very impressive. George Street offers five restaurants, all of them Chinese including the famous, Charlie Chans, Woo Sang and the Little Yang Sing. There are also two supermarkets, a food store and a hair salon on this street.

What's it all about?

It is not until it is pointed out that it becomes apparent that Chinatowns across Britain are generously served by Chinese-run hair salons. One of the reasons for this is that Chinese hair differs from European hair in that if you look at a cross section of Chinese hair it is shaped like a rugby ball, rather than European hair which is shaped like a football. The particular shape makes it grow very straight. This requires a particular skill to cut (so the hairstylist would argue) and equally to perm - a common request among both Chinese men and women who want to look different!

Memory Lane

George Street is named after King George II– and the neighbouring Charlotte Street after his queen– both built in 1784. The Church of St James was begun in 1786. It was eventually demolished in 1903. The site is now occupied by St James' House.

Benjamin Heywood lived at number 41 in 1816, Although a banker by profession, he founded the Mechanics Institute.

Joseph Ashead, prison reformer and founder of 'ragged schools' which gave education to poor children lived in George Street in the mid 1840s.

New Year Celebrations in Manchester: the Dragon moves lowly through the crowds in George Street.

The Imperial Arch as seen from Nicholas Street

The Imperial Arch is at the junction of George Street and Nicholas Street which is notable for its lack of Chinese restaurants! Only one of the ten Chinese businesses located here is a restaurant.

Most of the others are service industries, all housed in the rather strangely named T La Arts and Crafts Building. However, the Arts and Crafts shop is well worth a visit - having a strange mixture of the mundane, the fascinating and the bizarre.

Memory Lane

Nicholas Street is named after Sir Nicholas Mosley (as is neighbouring Mosley Street) Nicholas Mosley was a prosperous merchant, the first of the Mosley family to be Lord of the Manor of Manchester. His business prospered so much that he moved to London for a time to handle its affairs there. During this time he became Lord Mayor of London in 1599, and endeared himself to Queen Elizabeth I by raising funds for her army.

利物浦

未來憧憬之城

充滿歷史榮耀與

Liverpool's Chinese Arrive

There is some evidence of very primitive man dwelling in the area of Liverpool, including the Calder Stones in Wavertree. But nothing of any great significance is known about Liverpool until the arrival of William the Conqueror, and the compilation of the Domesday Book. The book records that a settlement called 'Lytherpool' had developed by 1086, albeit consisting of no more than a church, a tower and a few huts.

In 1207 King John granted Liverpool a charter, recognising its potential as a seaport. As well as granting Liverpool a charter, King John also established a weekly market and annual trade fair which gave the impetus for the area's trade to grow. Within a few years construction on a castle started, standing where the Queens Memorial now stands.

Liverpool's development was slow- even by the mid 1500s its population was under 500. It was as late as 1660 that a Customs House was built, and major work undertaken to build the docks, thereby ending reliance on the tides. The opening of the dock in 1715 heralded Liverpool's arrival as an international port of significance.

Liverpool flourished on one of the most shameful chapters in Britain's history- the slave trade. It has been estimated that 10 million slaves were taken to America via Liverpool. The profits from slavery were huge, and much of Liverpool's splendour was built on those profits. This ended in 1807 when Britain abolished its involvement with the evil trade.

By the nineteenth century Liverpool was rapidly expanding, once again developing a big business in the transportation of humans beings with around 9 million passengers voluntarily making the journey from Liverpool to the New World between 1830 and 1930. Profits were invested and reinvested, and grand buildings erected, streets remodelled, and the world's first passenger railway linking Liverpool and Manchester opened in 1830.

Reading the news outside number 9 Pitt Street, 1940

Shortly afterwards Liverpool's first Chinese arrived – although none are likely to have stayed. On the 12th June 1834 the *Duchess of Clarence*, belonging to John Bibby & Co, was the first ship not owned by the East India Company (who lost their monopoly the same year) to arrive in Liverpool from China. In addition to her cargo of tea, there were Chinese sailors on board. The first ship to sail back to China from Liverpool embarked six months later.

In 1880 Liverpool was granted City Status by Royal Charter. By this time Chinese sailors were to be seen regularly around the docks of Liverpool, London and Cardiff; indeed the start of Liverpool's permanent Chinese community probably dates to around 1870 with the establishment in 1868 of a direct shipping service between Britain and China.

Such was the level of activity that China decided to establish an Embassy in Britain. The first officials arrived in Liverpool in September 1868 and processed in what must have been a spectacular display from the docks to the Adelphi Hotel. On sight of the Chinese (although China had appointed an American citizen as its Ambassador), the Adelphi Hotel refused the party entrance, the local paper euphemistically citing a 'misunderstanding' as the problem. This is possibly the first recorded case of race discrimination against the Chinese in Britain.

The Chinese settled around the dock area, most notably on Cleveland Square, Pitt Street and Frederick Street. Relations with the locals appears to have been very good, the area having a long history of immigrant communities.

As a result of an article by Claude Blake entitled "Chinese Vice in England" in the *Sunday Chronicle* in December 1906 anti-Chinese feeling spread, so much so that the council set up a commission to investigate the Chinese community. It defined Chinatown as the whole of the immediate neighbourhood of Cleveland Square and the adjoining streets.

Liverpool's Chinese Arrive

Despite the slurs of the *Chronicle*, the findings of the commission proved very positive towards the Chinese, and echoed the words of the *Chronicle's* rival, *The Courier*, which, in November 1906 had said "It is noteworthy that from the earliest years of their settlement, the Chinese have been regarded as the embodiment of public order".

By the 1930s Liverpool's total population had grown to over 800,000. The Chinese community were by now well established, with Chinatown situated in the heart of the old docks, and what would be called today an area of "inner city need". Forty-four of Pitt Street's 58 addresses were listed as being Chinese houses, shop, restaurants, laundries and associations.

At the end of the 1930s Liverpool council decided to demolish Pitt Street and much of the surrounding area, and to redevelop it. What was not destroyed by the city council was finished off by the German Luftwaffe during World War II.

With the demise of Pitt Street the Chinese began to move out into the suburbs, with a few moving to Nelson Street and George Square where the shipping company Holts, had established a new seaman's hostel to replace the boarding houses lost in Pitt Street and Cleveland Square. From here Chinatown grew "organically" to take in (to a greater or lesser extent) Berry Street, Duke Street and Upper Parliament Street.

Today Chinatown is still centred on Nelson Street and Berry Street. It has to be said, Chinatown has seen better times, but then, so has Liverpool. The size of the Chinese community has shrunk with many moving to more economically active areas such as Manchester and Birmingham.

Nonetheless, there are hopes of a brighter future. In January 2000 the new Imperial Arch was opened, marking a new phase in Chinatown's development. Proposals to restore and move the Chinese Pavillion and Pagoda from the 1984 International Garden Festival site to Chinatown would confirm Liverpool (architecturally speaking) as Europe's most spectacular Chinatown.

Getting There

Situated in the southern corner of the city centre, Liverpool's Chinatown is easily reached on foot from anywhere within the city centre area.

Driving to Liverpool's Chinatown is also easily achieved, with pay and display bays on both Berry Street and Nelson Street.

National Rail & Merseyrail

For National Rail, Lime Street Station serves Liverpool, and is a 10 to 15 minute walk from Chinatown. Exit onto Lime Street and turn left, past the Adelphi Hotel and onto Renshaw Street which eventually becomes Berry Street

For Merseyrail, the nearest station is Central Station, and about 10 minutes away. Exit onto Bold Street, turn right and walk to the top of the street. Berry Street is on the right.

Coach

The National Coach station is situated on Norton Street. Walk down London Road onto Lime Street and follow the directions as per National Rail above.

Bus

Because it is so central, any bus into the city centre will be close enough to walk to Chinatown. From Wiliamson Square walk through the Clayton Square Shopping centre, take the Church Street exit and turn left. Cross Ranelagh Street onto Bold Street and Berry Street is at the top .

Mersey Travel Line
0151 236 7676

LIVERPOOL
the world in one city

It's no wonder that Liverpool is bidding to be European Capital of Culture in 2008 – it is quite literally 'a world in one city'.

LIVERPOOL is home to one of the oldest and largest Chinese communities in Europe – much of it clustered amidst some of the most stunning architecture and famous locations.

The city has a magnificent cultural offer with more art galleries and museums than any other UK city outside London including the Walker, the internationally acclaimed gallery and Tate Liverpool, the only Tate Gallery in Northern Britain. All just a short distance from the focal point of Liverpool's Chinatown – the largest Chinese Arch outside China.

Liverpool is famous as the birthplace of the Beatles and you won't be disappointed taking a tour that includes Penny Lane and Strawberry Fields, or visiting the Beatles museum in the famous Albert Dock.

Take some time for sport – either watching one of the premier clubs – Liverpool or Everton, or playing on one of the many golf courses giving the region the title of "England's Golfing Capital".

And at the end of the day, Liverpool comes alive with a huge choice of restaurants, café bars and – as you would expect in one of the UK's great party cities – a wide range of live music venues offering bands, groups and artists seven days a week!

www.visitliverpool.com

liverpool
TOURIST INFORMATION CENTRE

LIVERPOOL 2008
EUROPEAN CAPITAL OF CULTURE BID

make it merseyside

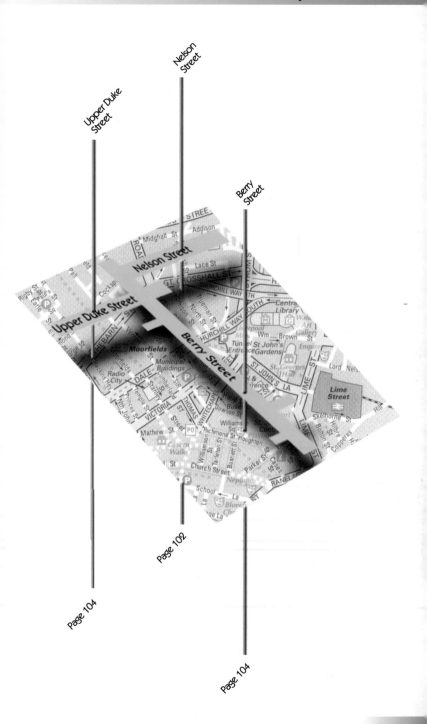

Upper Duke Street

Nelson Street

Berry Street

Page 102

Page 104

Page 104

*Liverpool's Imperial Arch
- the largest outside of China.*

The year 2000 saw many new landmarks appearing across Britain - the Millennium Dome and the Tate Modern in London, and The Eden Project in Cornwall. All impressive, but the Chinese Archway in Liverpool must rank among the most spectacular.

The archway is situated at the east end of Nelson Street, with the arch actually spanning the street. It's difficult to explain the sheer scale of this archway, the largest outside of China. It stands 15 metres-or some 50 feet-tall. That's impressive on paper, but standing next to it, it's quite staggering. The white marble blocks on which each of the four supports stand are 2 metres high (6 and a half feet) and as the eye is drawn up to

the five roofs it is the complexity of the joinery combined with the exuberance of the decoration which makes Liverpool's arch so awesome. There are in fact no fewer than 200 dragons painted, carved and gilded, onto this structure. The whole structure is protected on its eaves by eight fearsome dragon heads as well as a collection of other guardian creatures. Unsurprisingly the Archway won the Architectural and Tourism Award.

The archway was shipped from Shanghai in China piece by piece. Once in the UK it was constructed by craftsmen from Shanghai, construction work starting on 26th November 1999. The arch was finally completed on 31th January 2000, just in time to celebrate the Chinese New Year of the Dragon. As all the work was undertaken under a covering: the eventual unveiling must have been spectacular.

The idea of an archway in Chinatown was first mooted back in the 1980s. The archway is the outcome of years of co-operation and co-ordination between the Liverpool Chinatown Business Association, Liverpool City Council, Liverpool Rope Walks Partnership and The Liverpool Chamber of Commerce and Industry.

Zhong Guo Cheng - Chinatown

In the very centre of the archway are three characters. These alone are almost a metre in height. They read from left to right *Zhong Guo Cheng* - so simple a statement that it is almost ironic: "Chinatown".

To each side there are two panels. Again, scale is difficult to convey well, but each covers an area of 4 square metres containing two intricately carved dragons which have then been gilded.

The positioning of the Imperial Arch is said to have been governed by the principles of feng shui. Indeed, feng shui may have been consulted, but its difficult to imagine that the archway could really have been built anywhere else.

The archway sits in a landscaped area, although most of the landscaping is "hard". Sitting at the front of the archway are two bronze lions, traditional guardians of temples and building of importance in China (see page 101).

There is a seating area on the right hand side of the archway (as facing it), and easily missed are the Chinese characters which are incorporated into the iron lattice work. These are read from the pavement side of the seating area, (illustrated at the bottom of page 103) and read *Si Hai Yi Jia Minzhu Gonghe Caiyuan Shengli Yulong*.

This is a poetic statement, and does not easily translate - but approximately it reads:

From across the seven seas people came and united, bringing prosperity and commercial success.

Lions

There are six lions which guard the entrances to Chinatown. Two guard each end of Nelson Street, while one pair protect the approach to Chinatown from the City Centre.

Unlike other Chinatowns, the lions in Liverpool are not made of stone, but are rather made of bronze, with a male and a female lion (see *What's it all about?*, page 109) sitting atop of brick podiums.

Each podium has a four character Chinese text on it with the pair at the front of the Imperial Archway having the same inscription as is found on the pair which guard the approach into Chinatown on Berry Street.

The four inscriptions, with transliteration and translations are shown below.

華洋並重
Hua Yang Bing Zhong
Equality between Chinese and Europeans

埠郡齊興
Bu Jun Qi Xing
Prosperity to the city and county

神恩永眷
Shen En Yong Juan
Eternal spirit of kindness

主愛長存
Zhu Ai Chang Cun
Eternal spirit of love

One interesting note is the use of both the traditional word for "spirit" and the Christian word. "Eternal spirit of love" uses the Christian word (zhu), and "Eternal spirit of kindness" the traditional Chinese word (shen).

What's it all about?

The lion is not native to China, so it may be a little surprising how prevalent this animal is in Chinese culture. Equally, this may explain why Chinese lions are so far removed from realistic depictions of the animals. The Chinese word for lion is *Shizi* which it is thought comes from the Persian for lion, *sir*. If this is the case, then the first lions to enter China may well have been as gifts from ambassadors from western Asia – it is known that imperial zoos existed thousands of years ago. The lion's importance, however, is undoubtedly derived from India and its place in Buddhist thought, figuring as it does as the defender of law and protector of sacred buildings. This is the origin of the stone lions in front of temples and tombs. The depiction is not realistic, and these lions were historically mistaken as dogs by westerners who called them *Fu Dogs* - Fu being a transliteration of *Fo* meaning Buddhist.

In traditional Chinese statues of lions, they are always seated, either with both front feet on the ground, or one raised, the latter probably a pose of defence. Often the lions are depicted as having either a lion cub under the right paw or a ball under the left paw. The lion with a cub under the paw is female, while the ball only accompanies the male lion (a lion may have a ball under the left paw if two male lions are guarding a building). The presence of the ball is quite interesting, as such balls are associated with mythical beasts, the prime example being the dragon. As only a handful of Chinese would have actually seen a lion, it is not hard to understand why it may have been believed to be a mythical creature.

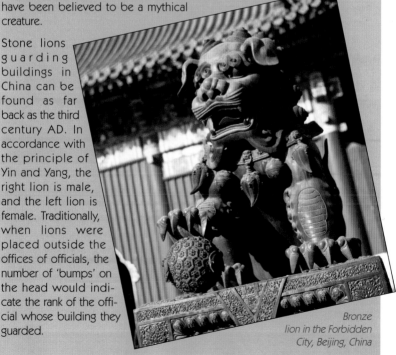

Stone lions guarding buildings in China can be found as far back as the third century AD. In accordance with the principle of Yin and Yang, the right lion is male, and the left lion is female. Traditionally, when lions were placed outside the offices of officials, the number of 'bumps' on the head would indicate the rank of the official whose building they guarded.

Bronze lion in the Forbidden City, Beijing, China

Nelson Street is the heart of Liverpool's Chinatown, and its significance is celebrated by the abundance of Chinese street furniture, all against the backdrop of the archway.

Of all of Britain's Chinatowns, Liverpool, it has to be said, has managed to landscape the area with exuberance, yet without making the area seem like a village at Disneyland. The fact that there are no telephone kiosks with plastic pagoda-style roofs is a definite plus. The bollards, lamp posts and even the dustbins all blend to form a co-ordinated feel which in some way seems lacking in other Chinatowns.

Number One Nelson Street is actually the Pine Court Housing Association. Nothing very Chinese sounding about that, although the Association does have a focus on providing housing for the local Chinese Community, though not exclusively. It also acts as a training resource for those seeking to enter into the housing field. It certainly ensures that Liverpool Chinatown is actually a place where people live, and not just a commercial centre.

This really sets the stage for Nelson Street - it holds a fascinating collection of places, from the Nook Pub - complete with its own sign in Chinese which declares it the country's first

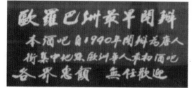

Chinese local, dating back to 1940, to the home of the Chinese Freemason's, two community associations, and, of course Chinese restaurants - in fact they total ten in all.

At the end of Nelson Street is George Square, in which Britain's oldest Chinese Christian congregation is based.

One of Nelson's Street's most intriguing buildings is to be found at number 22. Intriguing because it is unashamedly baffling to the non-Chinese reader, but clearly has a message to tell. It's the See Yep Association. Black granite is carved with characters painted in gold, and its difficult not to wonder what this

important message is. The characters down either side of the front door form a couplet, and read from the right had side first. Couplets can be regarded as a form of poetry, and literal translation difficult. This is a particulalry complex poem, with the two texts having a complex matching character system. For example, the first characters from each text reads "See Yep" (the Association name) Subsequent pairs are linked in various ways. Chinatown Britian provides you with a (very) liberal translation.

Right Side
Old friends gather and peace and prosperity follows

Left Side
Great prosperity and fortune follow wherever old friends reunite.

Traditional colours of luck and prosperity have been used for Liverpool's Street furniture, with the street bollards carrying the Chinese characters "Jixiang" which means Good Luck. Clearly someone wanted to take no chances!

Berry Street was once of greater significance than it is today, with a number of Chinese businesses running off onto the side street. However, with the decline in population, and the general decay in Liverpool Chinatown, these businesses have not only closed, but many of the buildings have become derelict. In truth this is probably just a reflection of the wider story of Liverpool's decline during the 80s.

That said, there are still a significant number of businesses on Berry Street, including the enormous "buffet style' Far East restaurant - one of Liverpool's oldest. Of course, cheaper rents means that a wider selection of businesses can be supported, and it's well worth going into some of the arts and crafts type stores - you never know what unusual treasure you could walk out with.

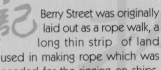

Memory Lane

拾
遺
記

Berry Street was named after Henry Berry, Liverpool's second dock engineer who lived in a house on Duke Street.

Berry Street was originally laid out as a rope walk, a long thin strip of land used in making rope which was needed for the rigging on ships. At its height, there were over a dozen "ropewalks" in Liverpool.

Upper Duke Street
Upper Duke Street is Liverpool Chinatown's third street in terms of significance, though that said, there's only a few businesses there, the most important of which is the supermarket.

LIVERPOOL
the world in one city

Planning your visit to Liverpool

Liverpool offers you a wide choice of where to stay – from a range of 4 star hotels, including the International Marriott hotels and Crowne Plaza, to youth hostels and self-catering accommodation at competitive rates.

For a quick, easy (and free) way to book in advance of your visit call Liverpool Tourist Information's Reservation Service. Friendly staff will help you find the perfect place to stay at the price you want to pay.

0845 601 1125
outside UK (+44) 151 709 8111

Or book online at
www.visitliverpool.com

liverpool
TOURIST INFORMATION
CENTRE

LIVERPOOL 2008
EUROPEAN CAPITAL OF CULTURE BID

make it merseyside

Birmingham
City of Renewal

伯明翰

萬象新興之城

Birmingham's history can be traced back to Roman Britain, with Roman remains having been discovered in the leafy suburb of Edgbaston. By the time of the Domesday Book there was a settlement in the Bull Ring area which was valued at 20 shillings. King Henry II gave William de Bermingham a charter in 1166 which allowed him to hold a market on its land. This was extended in 1250 by Henry III to include a fair for merchants, and so began Birmingham's development as a commercial centre.

By 1550 the population of Birmingham was about 1500, but over the next 150 years the population grew substantially so that by 1700 there were around 15,000 inhabitants. One hundred and fifty years more, and the population had exploded to over 70,000 as the city became the cradle of the Industrial Revolution.

Today Birmingham's Chinatown lies in the Deritend district of the city, adjacent to the city's indoor market – the legacy of William de Bermingham. Perhaps because it was in a wet, swampy area, Deritend was never the first choice for development. Today's Chinatown, nestling as it does between trendy bars and clubs and the city's gay village belies the humble origins of this area of the city.

The rather run down area of Deritend became home to immigrant Jews - it is recorded that a Jewish synagogue existed in "The Froggery", probably a reference to the swampy nature of the area. As the Industrial Revolution took hold, Birmingham saw mass migration, not only from the surrounding countryside and nearby towns, but also from abroad. By 1818 the Deritend area had become known as Little Italy. An Italian community prospered in the area, and at its height in 1915 there were between 600 and 700 Italians living in Little Italy. With their growing success and affluence the Italian community moved into the more upmarket district of Aston. During the Second World War, many Italians were sent to internment camps on the Isle of Man. Despite large scale Italian immigration in the post war years, Little Italy disappeared.

The area became run down and dilapidated. What may come as something of a surprise is that the first Chinese restaurant to open in Birmingham opened as late as 1959, called the Tung Hing, in the Snow Hill area of the city, a short walk from

In May 1906 a delegation led by Duke Tse Tsai– pictured here at the Metro Camel railway works in Birmingham– visited the UK for the "study of western government and the study of industrial methods"

Deritend, and the present day location of Chinatown.

When Birmingham's first Chinese restaurant opened in 1959 (pictured below) there were fewer than 20 Chinese people in the whole of the West Midlands. Being as far away from any port as you can get in Britain, the Chinese moved in through a process of "economic migration". The size of Birmingham's population coupled with the scarcity of Chinese people made the city an ideal location for those prepared to move to enjoy the boom in Chinese catering.

It was in Hurst Street that Birmingham's first Chinese community Centre was established. Although the words 'community centre' may conjure up images of quite organised facilities, Birmingham's first Chinese community centre also doubled as a beansprout factory!

The Tung Hing restaurant in 1957

Getting There

Birmingham's Chinatown is situated in the very heart of the city, and neighbours both the nightclub district and the gay village.

Car parking is easy as there is a large car park on Hurst Street, as well as a multistorey indoor car park above the new indoor markets. In addition there is the car park beneath the Arcadian Centre and some street parking. All car parks are signposted.

By Rail

Birmingham New Street National Rail station is just a 5 minute walk away. Exit the station by the main entrance (do not go up the escalators into the Palladian Shopping Centre). Walk to the main road and turn right. Twenty metres down the road there are stairs to the street level below. At the bottom of the stairs turn left and Chinatown is a short distance straight ahead.

By Coach

Digbeth Coach station is 5 minutes walk from Chinatown. Exit onto Digbeth High Street, turn left, take the second left (Upper Dean St), the Arcadian Centre is at the top of this street.

By Bus

With such a central location there are dozens of buses that come within walking distance of Chinatown. Any bus going to New Street can be used, and the directions from the train station followed.

Centro - West Midlands Passenger Transport Authority
0121 200 2700

點止
雜貨舖咁簡單

Wing Yip
All the Chinese you need to know

Head Office:

375 Nechells Park Road
Nechells, Birmingham
B7 5NT

Tel: 0121 327 6618
Fax: 0121 327 6612

395 Cricklewood Road
Cricklewood, London
NW2 6LN

Tel: 020 8450 0422

Oldham Road
Ancoats, Manchester
M4 5HU

Tel: 0161 832 3215

544 Purley Way
Croydon, London
CR0 4NZ

Tel: 020 8688 4880

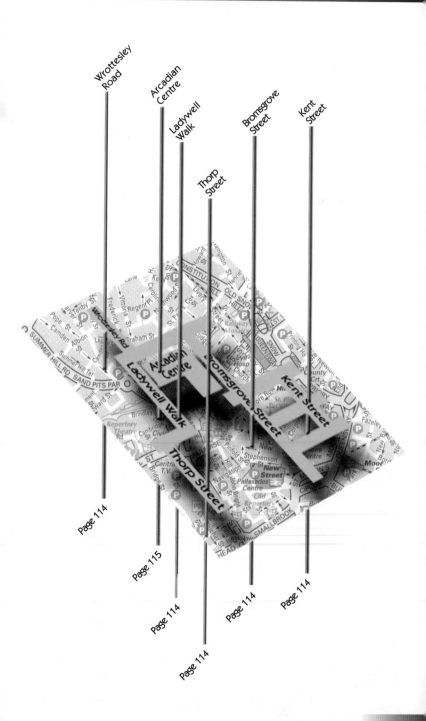

Wrottesley Road

Arcadian Centre

Ladywell Walk

Thorp Street

Bromsgrove Street

Kent Street

Page 114

Page 115

Page 114

Page 114

Page 114

Page 114

Damage caused by bombing during the Second World War allowed Birmingham City Council to take radical action when redeveloping the city centre, and a wide sweeping road system was introduced, as well as the building of the now demolished Bull Ring Centre. This redevelopment also gave the opportunity to rid the city of many slum areas. One of the great new projects was the Colmore Circus, the crossroads for the northern approach to the city with the new ring road.

The post-war town planners could not have imagined that in less than 40 years, their new world of concrete underpasses and flyovers would be dominated by Britain's only genuine Chinese pagoda.

Carved in Fujian Province of Chinese granite, the 12.5m pagoda was a donation to the city from the Chinese entrepreneur, Mr Wing Yip, whose food import and distribution empire first began in a modest shop in Digbeth, just a stone's throw from Chinatown.

The design is based on traditional principles, and the numerology of the structure is evident in the eight sides of the structure. In Chinese culture the number eight is considered very auspicious, as its sound is similar to the Chinese word for luck (such numerological considerations can also be seen in items such as the eight sided ba gua mirror used in feng shui, see page 113). There are seven storeys, and though the reasons are lost in the mists of time, all pagodas in China either have seven or nine storeys.

The landscaping of the surrounding area was undertaken by the City of Birmingham, partly funded by the European Union, with the landscaping based on feng shui principles.

What's it all about?

Many of China's cultural treasures have been exported and are now better known as arts of the recipient countries: for example, bonzai cultivation is Chinese in origin not Japanese and tea originated not in India, but China. The pagoda however is a major exception. The pagoda is of Indian origin, and was probably imported into China along with Buddhism in the first century AD.

Pagodas were originally built to house religious artifacts and documents, to commemorate important events or to store the ashes of the dead. They later came to be used for purely ornamental reasons as well, and often combined to provide a high point to view the surrounding area.

A Pagoda in Shanghai.

Ladywell Walk is dominated by the Chung Ying and China Court restaurants with their Chinese architectural roofs. In the absence of any Chinese street furniture (Birmingham is the only Chinatown in Britain not to feature it) these landmark buildings let everyone know they have arrived in Chinatown.

Ladywell Walk has a number of other businesses, though it has to be said, it lacks the intimacy of Britain's other main Chinatown streets because it is very exposed and open. Perhaps it's a lack of hustle and bustle, or maybe the orderliness (there are no vegetables on upturned cartons spilling out into the street!) that make it all feel a little bit "softer" than London or Manchester. The relative tranquillity may be welcome, however, after experiencing shopping on Gerrard or Nelson Street.

The food of Birmingham may not be as well known as that of Manchester or London, but it more than holds its own against the best of both of these cities.

In addition to the restaurants Ladywell Walk sports a travel agency, Chinese herbalist, telephone store and supermarket.

Bromsgrove Road
Bromsgrove Road intersects with Hurst Street (off Ladywell Walk, but effectively a continuation of Ladywell Walk), a little past the Arcadian Centre. It offers a little cluster of three smaller restaurants.

Kent Street
Kent Street is home to the Far East Building. This is a commercial centre for Chinese service industries including a printers, accountants, communications company, a food factory and others.

Thorp Street
Again, a small side street, this time off Hurst Street. Has a large restaurant and a travel agents, with a financial services company a little further up the road. At the very top of the street is the Birmingham branch of the Bank of China

Wrottesley Street
A little side street off Ladywell Walk offers one of two branches of the Day On supermarket (the other being in the Arcadian Centre), a travel agency and a restaurant.

The Arcadian Centre is a leisure complex with a bit of a twist. In addition to twelve bars, a cinema, a comedy club and a hotel, it is also home to over a dozen Chinese businesses.

The centre was built in the heart of Chinatown which for many years had been a backwater. It may have been inevitable that Chinatown would spill over into the new development, but interestingly it has gone well beyond that and become an intrinsic part of it. The parade of shops within the Arcadian Centre is known as Cathay Street. It's well worth a peek because there are lots of the service industries here, from accountants to bakers, booksellers to gift shops, supermarkets to hairdressers.

The central plaza area also provides a natural arena for the Chinese New Year celebrations of Birmingham's Chinese community.

What's it all about?

Cathay is an old European name for China dating from about 1250 when it was used by Marco Polo. It is derived from the mediæval latin *Cataya*, taken from the 10th century Turkic word applied to the Manchurian Tartar kingdom of *Kitai*.

The Armenian geographer Het'um The Historian, described the land of Cathay in the 14th century:

"The Kingdom of Cathay is the most noble and rich realm in the world. It is full of people and limitless grandeur, and is located by the shore of the Ocean. There are so many islands in the sea that it is impossible to count them. Now the people are rich with countless luxuries and treasures."

The modern Russian word for China, *Kitay*, still reflects the original Turkic source.

新堡

蘊美之城

Newcastle
City of Hidden Beauty

Newcastle's Chinese Arrive

The Romans built a bridge across the River Tyne, and a small fort to guard it, called 'Pons Aelius' – the Bridge of the Emperor Aeliusm Hadrian Aelius better known for having built Hadrian's Wall. The fort also defended the eastern end of the wall.

In Anglo-Saxon times it had become known as Monkchester, on account of a small friary. The name Newcastle came about after Robert Curthose, eldest son of William the Conqueror built a castle here on return from a raid into Scotland in 1080.

Robert's "new castle" became the defacto place name for the place, with the castle being built precisely on the site of Pons Aelius, and is now the location of the Castle Keep.

It is not surprising that a town

grew around the castle, around which a wall was built as a defence from the Scots. Today the best surviving example of these walls is behind Chinatown's Stowell Street.

Newcastle's military significance gave rise to commercial importance, and its proximity to the sea lead to the development of one of Britain's most important sea ports. By 1400, its importance was such that Newcastle became a county in its own right.

Several important industries such as rope making, shipbuilding and glass making developed, but of greatest importance was Newcastle's coal mining industry, supplying coal to London by sea. Although mined outside of the city, Newcastle's port was the only one capable of handling the coal, and so it became the regional centre for transporting coal. So synonymous did Newcastle become with coal, that the phrase `To carry coals to Newcastle', was coined.

The monopoly that Newcastle developed brought in a great deal of wealth to the city. With this wealth the city was redesigned and built largely by one man – Richard Grainger. The central district of the town is now known as Grainger Town. In just five years, Richard Grainger transformed the centre of Newcastle into an astounding display of classical beauty. Chinatown lies in the northwest of Grainger Town, centred on Stowell

Stowell Street, 1969

Street. Stowell Street was built parallel to the town walls in 1824, and broke 300 years of history by encroaching on the Blackfriar's precinct. Soon the whole area was developed, though surprisingly most of the Blackfriar's buildings remain intact to this day.

The arrival of the Chinese in Newcastle in any number can only be traced back about three decades, a much later development than Liverpool, London or Manchester. The entry was by natural migration, usually in search of business opportunities. Opportunities in the catering industry had the effect of dispersing the Chinese, first to the larger cities, but eventually to any town or even village of any size.

The first Chinese restaurant in Newcastle opened in 1949 in Scotswood Road, called the Marlbrough Cafe. It caused something of a stir by opening seven days a week.

Getting There

Newcastle's Chinatown lies in the northwest corner of the city centre, and is easily reached on foot from any cental location. Signposts throughout the city centre point the way.

Car parking in the area is fairly abundant and signposted.

By Rail

Newcastle's Central Station is a ten minute walk away. Exit the station by the main entrance and cross the road (Neille Street) and walk up Pink Lane (cross Clayton Street West and continue up the lane). At the end of Pink lane, Cross Street, and the start of Chinatown is on the opposite side of Westgare Road, or cross Westgate Road, turn left into Bath Lane, and Stowell Street is the first on the right.

By Coach

Gallowgate coach station is just two minutes walk from Chinatown. Simply turn into St Andrew's Road and Stowell Street is first right.

By Bus and Metro

With such a central location there are dozens of buses that come close enough to Chinatown to walk to. Any bus going to Central Station can be used, and the directions from the train station followed. St James Metro serves Gallowgate Coach station, and is just a few minutes away. Follow the Coach Station direction.

Newcastle Tourist Information
0191 277 8000

from 10 am to 11 pm. A three course lunch was available at a cost of a shilling and threepence. There was an estimated Chinese population in the Northeast of just 30 people in 1949.

By 1962 there were 15 Chinese restaurants in Newcastle, none of them in Stowell Street. As the Chinese population grew, the North East Chinese Association was founded in 1979, moving to its present home on Stowell Street in 1983.

The development of Stowell Street as a Chinese quarter only goes back to 1982. Up to this time Stowell Street had been a rather rundown unfashionable street – ideal for Chinese entrepreneurs looking for low rents but access to a large market.

"Truly the Chinese can claim to have brought Stowell Street back to life, for whereas at the end of the 1970s it was a dreary area with almost every building dilapidated, now it is thriving and one of the city's most popular eating places."

Peter Chan
A Sampan's Journey

In 1982 a small nucleus of Chinese establishments had formed in Stowell Street. – the Jade Garden Restaurant (Stowell Street's first), the Wing Hong supermarket, an Arts and Crafts shop above the Jade garden and a travel agents. In the same year the Newcastle Journal reported:

"It's a little premature to attach the label 'Chinatown' to Stowell Street, but things are looking that way."

Newcastle Journal
25 September 1982

By 1991 Stowell Street had come of age as Chinatown with the arrival of a pair of Stone Lions from Xi'an, China. The lions were positioned by a feng shui expert , and were a gift to to the city from restaurateur, Barry Yu.

At the same time the Dragon and Phoenix mural was constructed on the side of the North East Chinese Association building, with the original cost being met by the City Council, and its maintenance paid for by the Chinese community.

In 1994 Mascot House opened, at the top of Stowell Street, a sheltered housing scheme for elderly Chinese. At the time it was quite revolutionary, as "City Centre Living" had yet to be discovered, and many wondered why a new development would be built in a city centre location.

Chinatown grew from strength to strength, and the Chinese population expanded. The success of Chinatown came under its greatest threat in 2001 when "a Chinese restaurant" in the North East was linked to the cause of Britain's foot and mouth disease outbreak. The story was carried in broadsheet newspapers and tabloids alike, with the notable exception of *The Independent.* The papers quoted a source from the Ministry of Agriculture Fisheries and Food. The Chinese of Britain were outraged, and following the largest demonstrations by Chinese in British history. Nick Brown, the Agriculture Minister made a public denial of the claims. The damage to Chinese businesses was, however done, and millions of pounds in lost trade suffered.

The Mural on Stowell Street was erected in 1991, paid for by the City Council as part of a wider plan to follow the success of other Chinatowns in making the area more attractive to tourists.

Originally it stood on the side of the North East Chinese Association building; however, with the development of The Gate Shopping Centre, the mural was moved to the side of the Co-Operative carpark.

The mural depicts a dragon and a phoenix, and represents harmony. At night it is illuminated with neon lights.

The dragon is a Chinese symbol of authority and power. It was an emblem of the Emperor.

The phoenix is a symbol of peace and prosperity. It is seen as the "opposite" of the dragon in sense of

Yin and Yang; therefore whereas the dragon is very masculine, the phoenix is seen as feminine. Together the dragon and phoenix represent harmony, balance and peaceful co-existence.

The dragon and phoenix theme can often be seen in restaurants, particularly as a backdrop to a low platform. These platforms are use as the setting for the "top table" at weddings - with the bride and groom sitting in front of the dragon and phoenix representing marital harmony.

The clouds above the dragon and phoenix may seem odd, but in fact the dragon is a flying creature - the Chinese consider the dragon to be the "king of the skies".

The mural is maintained by the local Chinese community.

Stowell Street is named after Lord Stowell, the brother of Lord Eldon (of Eldon Square). The street began life back in 1824, and was built across open land which had belonged to Blackfriars monastery for over 300 years. It was the first street to be built here, but once established, the surrounding area was also soon developed. The original street was entirely made up of artisans houses, though most of these have now been lost.

Memory Lane

The buildings of 38-46 Stowell Street are the best preserved original buildings from 1824.

14-18 Stowell Street is a rather impressive building, particularly given that it was originally a warehouse and offices for the Co-Operative Society. Originally built in 1908.

Newcastle Town Walls

During a visit to Newcastle's Chinatown it is worth taking a few minutes to take a look at the old town walls. The walls date back more than 700 years. Probably the most impressive view of the walls lies at the top of Stowell Street. Along the walls were various towers, and the tower at the top of modern Stowell Street is not only one of the best preserved, but also one of the most important, being at the junction of the wall where it makes a right angle turn. The tower is called Heber tower.

The towers were occupied in the 18th century by the various Guilds (there were 17 towers in all). Heber Tower was occupied by the Currier Guild (people who coloured leather), with Feltmakers and Armourers.

There is a small doorway to the right of the tower which was made in 1810 as a means of improving access to a number of city institutions which were outside of the city walls, most notably the hospital, poor house and lunatic asyslum.

Today this access point seems a little strange, given the large dry moat on the other side of the wall. However, in 1810, there was no moat here. It was redug as part of a restoration of the setting of the walls - it's an ideal place for a picnic in the summer months.

If you feel inspired by the Herber Tower, its worth taking a little look at the Morden Tower, which is behind the restaurants of Stowell Street.

As you walk along the wall you will be able to see the best preserved turrets of the wall. Some way down is the original gate which the Blackfriars received a royal license to build in 1280, giving them access to land outside the town walls (look for the small plaque next to it).

Morden Tower itself is characterised by the overhanging upper storey, built by the Guild of Glaziers, Plumbers, Pewrterers and Painters at the turn of the 18th century, and is still in use today, by the Morden Tower Literary group which holds its meetings there.

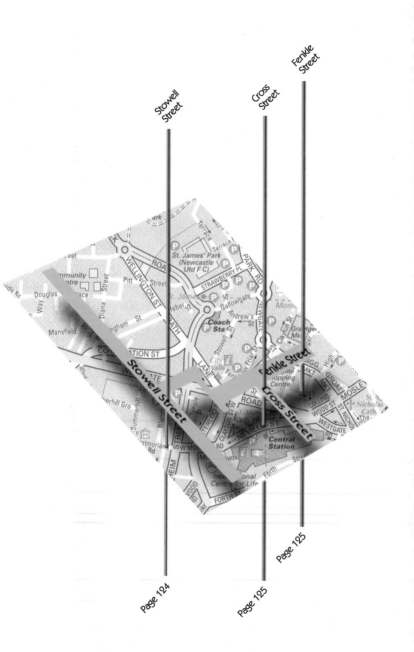

Stowell Street

Cross Street

Fenkle Street

Page 124

Page 125

Page 125

Stowell Street

Stowell Street is the very heart of Newcastle's Chinatown. Although Fenkle Street and Cross Street also have Chinese businesses, they can't compare in terms of the sheer number as well as variety of businesses to be found on Stowell Street.

The Chinese character of the street comes not only from the new facia and Chinese signage to the numerous shops and restaurants, but also from the street furniture which has been assembled as a co-operative work between the local community, city council and big business such as British Telecom and the Post Office. The Chinese lighting, post boxes, litter bins and "Chinese" fencing all add to a Chinese character, even though, it has to be said, it can seem at times a little forced. The worst offender in this sense was the mock Chinese roof that topped the carpark entrance. Such things are better done properly, and the wooden mock roof looked more like a leftover from an amateur dramatic society's production of Alladin than anything else. Fortunately it has gone, along with the mural and the stone lions from Xi'an.

There is some mystery as to what has happened to the lions, but doubtless, once the upheaval of the redevelopment of the area settles, they will reappear, much as the mural will.

There are many restaurants along Stowell Street, and something to match every budget. One of the newest arrivals is Mangos which provides an exciting modern interior with excellent food and service.

Wing Hong Supermarket was the first on Stowell Street, and has served the local community for almost 20 years. The wide range of both food and

non-food products makes this store probably the most interesting in Chinatown – browse through at your leisure, from the unusual Chinese ingredients through to ceramics and kitchenware, ornaments and greeting cards.

There's also a Chinese video club though this is likely to be of little u unless you understand Chinese.

The North East Chinese Association not open to the public, though oft they have photo exhibits outsic showing recent events held by t Association.

Cross Street and Fenkle Street are probably best described as enclaves of Chinatown being as they are little distance from Stowell Street. It is interesting to note that the services and stores in this area of Chinatown are non-restaurant based, and serve the Chinese community in a broader sense, either through direct services such as travel agencies, or the business community with meat and seafood wholesalers.

The Po Shing supermarket on Fenkle Street is one of Newcastle's oldest, and indeed, the Chinese presence in this area is much older than in Stowell Street.

If you fancy a tea break, try the Jasmine cake shop, where a variety of Chinese "cakes" are available. If you enjoy them, you can even take some home!

Memory Lane

The origins of the name Fenkle Street is unclear. Some claim it to be a corruption of the word "fennel "(the herb), while other believe the street is named after Nicholas Fenkle, a merchant who lived in Newcastle in 1577.

The Po Shing supermarket building stands on the corner of Cross Street and Fenkle Street dates back to the early 1800s, and until 1892 was a pub.

Cross Street was previously called Rotten Row.

Your name in Chinese

Names Translated
Birth signs • Scrolls

www.chinesetext.co.uk

A Brief Chronology
of the Chinese in Britain

1637 John Weddell attempts to establish trading links with China.

1687 Shen Fu-Tsung, a Chinese scholar, is brought to Britain by Jesuit Priest, Father Philip Couplet, who had come to recruit more missionaries for China.

1711 The East India company are permitted to establish an office in Canton and subsequently develop a craze in all things Chinese.

1782 The first record of Chinese seamen in Britain.

1800 The East India company find a solution to the massive trade deficit brought on by the craze for Chinese products - the export from India of opium to China. 100 tons are shipped in 1800.

1814 An Act of Parliament 1814 was passed compelling the East India Company to provide lodgings and basic essentials for Chinese and "Asiatic" sailors – while awaiting a new signing on. The barracks at King David's Fort, East London, were used for this purpose.

1830s The growing concerns of the Chinese authorities over the importation of opium, and its social effects on the population lead to efforts to enforce laws against the importation of opium which had been made illegal in China in 1729 by the Chinese Emperor, Yung Cheng

1839 Confiscated British-owned opium is destroyed in public.

1840 4,000 British troops are sent to China to force her to accept trade in opium in what becomes known as the first opium war.

1841 Chinese troops prove no match for the British army, and as part of the peace settlement, Hong Kong is ceded to Britain for ever.

1851 British census shows 78 Chinese living in Briain

1860 British and Chinese troops fight the Second Opium War as China continues to try to stop the drug being brought into China.

Kowloon and Stonecutters Island ceded to Britain as part of the peace settlement to the Second Opium War.

1861 British census shows 147 Chinese living in Britain.

1866 First direct steamship service between China and Europe links Liverpool and Canton. The service uses Chinese some Chinese sailors.

1868 China sends its first "Ambassador" to Britain, an American by the name of Anson Burlingham. Of a party of 31, 28 were Chinese. All were dressed in Chinese clothes. Claiming a misunderstanding in the booking, the Adelphi Hotel refuses to accommodate the party.

1871 The British census shows 202 Chinese living in Britain.

1877 Guo Song Dao is appointed as China's first minister to Britain and a legation is opened in Portland Place, London , China's Embassy to this day

1882 Wu Ting Fang is the first Chinese person to be admitted to the Bar (becomes a barrister).

1886 Yee Chin's is the first Chinese laundry in Liverpool.

1885 Britain's first Chinatowns emerge near London and Liverpool docks, with Chinese also in the ports of Cardiff and Bristol.

1898 The New Territories loaned to Britain on a 99 year lease

1901 British census shows 387 Chinese living in Britain.

Sun Yat Sen (later first President of the Chinese Republic) arrives in London where he is abducted and imprisoned in the Chinese legation. Sun Yat Sen got a message out to Sir James Cantlie, his former medical school professor, who alerted Scotland Yard, The London Times and the Foreign Office, and won his release. The incident shoots Sun Yat Sen to fame.

1902 Media first begin the use of the term Chinatown.

London's first Chinese laundry opens in Poplar, and is immediately stoned by a hostile crowd.

1906 The TUC denounce Chinese labour in South Africa saying it is 'preventing South Africa' becoming a white man's country. In Liverpool unemployed white dockers dressed as Chinese were paraded around the streets of Liverpool' as propaganda during the General Election campaign. The Labour Party leaders were attempting to focus attention on the fact that Chinese workers were being sent to work in South Africa while British workers were unemployed.

Images of Chinese are used in the General Election which 'aroused among very many of the voters an immediate hatred of the Mongolian racial type".

1907 The Liverpool Courier reports: "It is noteworthy that from the earliest years of their settlement, the Chinese have been regarded as the embodiment of public order".

Among fears of the moral effect of the Chinese, Liverpool City council hold an official investigation. Liverpool's Chief Constable's findings describe the Chinese as "quiet, inofensive and industrious people"

1908 Chinese Mutual Aid societies established in Liverpool and London.

1909 Angry at cheap Chinese labour, British seamen prevent them signing on in London, and a police escort is required to get the Chinese seamen back to their lodgings safely.

First recorded opening of a Chinese restaurant in Britain.

1909 Liverpool City Council reports: "Unfortunately part of the lure of the Chinaman consists in the notorious fact that he does not get drunk and does not beat his woman, which is more than can be said of many a native suitor."

British census shows 1,319 Chinese living in Britan, with 4,595 Chinese seamen in port on Census day.

1911 An enquiry is held in London into the moral impact of the Chinese. East End police are of the opinion that the Chinese do not engage in prostitution with English girls preferring to marry them and treat them well.

In Cardiff British seamen identify cheap Chinese labour as a threat "the Chinaman is not worth a toss as a seaman...his only claim to indulgence is that he is cheap." Angry mobs destroy 30 Chinese laundries.

The Qing Dynasty is overthrown and the Republic of China established.

British Government plans to introduce hundred of thousands of Chinese labourers are abandoned as a result of trade union protests.

1916 The Chinese Seamen's Welfare Centre was opens in Bedford Street, Liverpool

95,000 Chinese are recruited to assist in Britain's war effort in France.

1917 The Aliens Restriction Act, originally designed to stem the settlement of Jews in Britain is extended. The Chinese population in Britain begins to decline.

1919 Zhong Shan Mutual Aid Workers CLub is established to unite the Chinese in Britain, improve their working conditions and look after their welfare.

1921 British census shows 2,419 Chinese living in Britain.

1923 An article in the Empire News states: 'The fascination of the Oriental for many young girls owing to his industry, sobriety, courtesy and good nature has long been regarded here and in Leeds as a moral yellow peril.'

1927 Local press in Liverpool report the "dying atmosphere" of Chinatown as immigration restrictions continue to reduce the number of Chinese.

1931 The British census shows 1,934 Chinese living in Britain. There are a reported 450 Chinese students in British universities

1935 There are over 500 Chinese laundries in Britain.

1937 The first Chinese School is established in Middlefields, East London with 30 students.

20,000 Chinese seamen form the Chinese Merchant Seaman's Pool with its HQ in Liverpool as war fever sets in. Chinese crews work on convoy ships throughout the war.

1944 The Chung Hua Chow Pao (Chinese Weekly News) is started in Liverpool.

1945 The Illustrated News reports: "The heroism of Chinese sailors is beyond praise and a number have been decorated by the King for gallantry."

1945+ Large numbers of Chinese seamen are repatriated.

1949 The People's Republic of China is founded.

1950s Large numbers of Chinese begin to arrive, and spread form Liverpool to Manchester and eventually to Birmingham and other British cities.

1951 British census shows 12,523 Chinese living in Britain.

1957 Britain now has about 300 Chinese restaurants. The Chinese laundry is fast disappearing.

1961 British census shows 38,750 Chinese living in Britain.

Britain's first Chinese community Centre opens in Gerrard Street, London

1963 Britain's Chinese population includes 6,000 students, and 2,000 nurses.

Wives of Chinese workers arrive to join their husbands.

1971 British census shows 96,030 Chinese living in Britain. The census reveals over 25% of Chinese in Britain were born in the country.

1976 Soho is firmly established as the location of London's new Chinatown.

1980 Actor David Yip makes TV history appearing in the "The Chinese Detective"

1980's Several thousand ethnic Chinese from Vietnam arrive in Britain as part of the international effort to resettle *Vietnamese Boat People.*

1981 British census shows 154,363 Chinese living in Britain.

1982 *Sweet and Sour* by Timothy Mo, is nominated for the Booker Prize.

1983 London's Chinatown is pedestrianised, iron archways and a pavilion are installed.

1985 The British government plans to grant right of abode to 50,000 'key personnel' from Hong Kong following its return to China: some in the media raise the old spectre of the "Yellow Peril".

1987 The size of London Chinatown's New Year celebrations force it to move the main stage activities to neighbouring Leicester Square.

1991 British census shows 156,938 Chinese living in Britain.

1997 Hong Kong reverts to Chinese sovereignty.

1998 Manchester's Chinatown Archway is Europe's largest, and the Chinese confer Dragon City status on the city.

Chinese children are identified by the Office for Standards in Education as Britain's highest academic achievers.

1999 The Observer reports the Chinese are Britain's highest earning, best educated people in Britain with the highest level of car ownership and the lowest level of unemployment.

2000 Jiang Zemin, visits Britain, the first Chinese Premiere to do so.

58 Chinese die of suffocation in the back of a lorry while trying to enter the UK by ferry from Holland.

The first national organisation for British born Chinese is established through a website, www.britishbornchinese.org.uk.

Liverpool unveils Europe's largest Imperial Arch at a height of 15 metres.

2001 Around 1,000 Chinese demonstrate on the streets of London following unfounded press allegations that the outbreak of foot and mouth Disease originated from illegally imported meat in the Newcastle area.

The Chinese Civil Rights Action Group is established.

Michael Chan becomes Britain's first Chinese Life Peer, becoming Lord Chan of Oxton.

2002 The Chinese community successfully challenge the British Library over its presentation of the history of the East India Company during its exhibition *Trading Places*, forcing changes to the exhibition and the online material to reflect the human costs of the company's activities in China.

Sweet and Sour is named by the Restaurant Association as Britain's most popular dish.

Index

Index